hm

Study Skills Program
LEVEL A

Developed by the Study Skills Group

Author and Co-Editor:	Aostre Nancy Johnson
Author:	Susan Kuntz
Co-Editor and Senior Editor:	David Marshak
Editorial Board:	Kiyo Morimoto, former Director Bureau of Study Counsel Harvard University
	Jerome Pieh, Headmaster Milton Academy

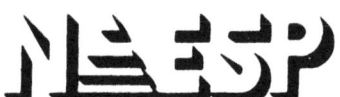 The National Association of Elementary School Principals
Alexandria, VA 22314

©Copyright 1990 by NATIONAL ASSOCIATION OF ELEMENTARY SCHOOL PRINCIPALS, 1615 Duke Street, Alexandria, Virginia 22314. All rights reserved. Manufactured in the United States of America. All hm Study Skills materials are copyrighted. No portion of this publication or its accompanying materials may be reproduced or copied, or stored in any information retrieval system, without the written permission of the NAESP.

ISBN: 978-0-8108-3811-6

NAESP 98765432

Illustrations: Judith Ruskin

TABLE OF CONTENTS

	INTRODUCTION	1
1	LISTENING	9
2	OBSERVING	23
3	UNDERSTANDING DIRECTIONS	39
4	CATEGORIES	56
5	PUT IT IN ORDER	72
6	PICTURES IN YOUR MIND	89
7	MAIN IDEA	101
8	CREATIVE PROBLEM SOLVING	113

INTRODUCTION TO THE hm STUDY SKILLS PROGRAM: LEVEL A

Dear Colleague:

The **hm Study Skills Program: Level A** is designed to provide you with a valuable resource for the teaching of study skills. Please read this Introduction carefully so you can gain a sense of the purposes and values, the means and ends, and the capacities and limitations of this program.

STUDY SKILLS: WHAT ARE THEY?

Study skills are learned abilities that one uses for the purpose of acquiring knowledge and competence. They are specific, observable behaviors that can be described and measured. For example, can a student attend to a set of directions and follow them accurately? Can a student identify the main idea of a story? Can a student think of a number of creative solutions to a problem?

Study skills can also be understood as *learning skills,* or *processes for learning.* They are processes that help students to organize and direct the effort they invest in learning. When students learn a study skill, they are learning how to learn more effectively. They are also learning how to take charge of their own learning.

THE hm STUDY SKILLS PROGRAM: LEVEL A

The **hm Study Skills Program: Level A** provides an introduction to fundamental study skills for students in grades 1 and 2 through a series of eight activity-oriented units.

The **hm Program** is structured on the assumption that activity-oriented lessons are the most effective way to teach study skills; more succinctly, that "learning by doing" is the best way to develop competence in study skills. The activities in the **hm Program** introduce students to basic learning skills that are useful in a wide variety of learning situations. Students then practice these skills in ways that (1) increase their awareness of the values of these skills and (2) help them become more conscious of themselves as learners.

The **hm Study Skills Program: Level A** provides you with a focus on the nature and value of skills that can help your students to become more effective learners. It gives you eight initial units for teaching study skills and a great many suggestions for further instruction and reinforcement in each study skill area.

The units in the **hm Study Skills Program: Level A** are:

1. Listening
2. Observing
3. Understanding Directions
4. Categories
5. Put It In Order
6. Pictures In Your Mind
7. Main Idea
8. Creative Problem Solving

THE DEVELOPMENTAL CHARACTER OF THE hm STUDY SKILLS PROGRAM: LEVEL A

The **hm Study Skills Program: Level A** is based on a developmental understanding of the capacities and needs of first and second graders. Children of these ages think differently than do older children, adolescents, or adults. They tend to be more holistic in their interaction with the world and experience the reality of their imaginations more vividly. They learn from their environment by observing, listening, manipulating objects, and moving their bodies.

The study skills presented in this **Program** are particularly appropriate for children of these ages. Some of these skills help children use their capacities to listen, observe, and visualize with greater intention and awareness. Other study skills help children begin to develop greater competence in such linear and analytic ways of thinking as sequencing and categorizing. Finally, children are encouraged to employ this whole repertoire of learning skills as they learn to solve problems more effectively and creatively.

Children in first and second grades are extremely varied in their readiness for formal reading and writing skills. The study skills in this program can all be effectively taught without relying on the ability to read or write.

STUDY SKILLS AND LEARNING STYLE

Research in cognitive and learning style during the past three decades has demonstrated what perceptive educators have known for a long time: people learn in very different and personal ways. Thus, study skills need to be taught in a way that helps children to value their own learning style(s) as they develop their skills for learning. Such instruction, guided by an awareness of individual differences, will help children to develop study skills that are specifically useful to their own capacities and needs.

The **hm Study Skills Program: Level A** is grounded in an awareness of learning style as a powerful factor in all learning. Its activities encourage students to find ways of learning that are effective for them as individuals.

USING THE hm STUDY SKILLS PROGRAM: LEVEL A

WHEN TO TEACH THE PROGRAM

Our field testing of the **hm Program: Level A** has shown that the vast majority of the activities in the **Program** are appropriate for first and second graders. However, when you are working with early first graders, you may want to give your students more guidance and take more time for some of the exercises.

READING AND WRITING SKILLS

The **Program** does not depend on the students' skills in reading and writing. There are printed words in the **Student Text** for those students who can read. However, teachers are directed in the **Teacher's Guide** to read aloud all of the material in the **Student Text**.

SEQUENCE OF INSTRUCTION

We have sequenced the eight units in the **Program** in an order that is developmentally sound and effectively balanced in terms of the diversity of the activities within the various units. We recommend that you use the units in the order in which they appear in the **Program**.

If you do choose to teach some units in a different sequence, you will want to keep the following in mind:

- Units 1, 2, and 3 are best taught as a cluster in the order in which they appear in the **Program**. Skills and concepts presented in Units 1 and 2 provide a foundation for the activities in Unit 3.

- Units 4, 5, and 7 are the most academically demanding units and contain more conventional workbook exercises than the other units. You may want to teach these units after your students are comfortable with the **Program's** format.

- Units 6 and 8 tie together many of the skills and concepts presented in the earlier units as well as presenting imagination and creativity as fundamental skills essential to the learning process.

PACING OF INSTRUCTION

No one pacing for the teaching of these units can be recommended for all classes. We have learned from the field test of the **Program** that teachers must pace the use of these units in a way that helps their particular students to acquire competence in the various skills.

Each unit is structured so that the basic activities can be presented in one week. Therefore, the entire **Program** could be presented in eight weeks.

A pacing that many of our field testers used with success was to begin a new unit every two weeks. During the first week of each two week cycle, they taught the activities in each unit in the **Program**. During the second week they gave their students ongoing practice of the new skills by engaging them in selected activities from each unit's *Additional Suggestions*.

We recommend that you conduct these kinds of follow-up activities to help your students develop the study skills introduced to them in each unit. We also urge you *to integrate the practice of study skills into your regular curriculum whenever possible*. The *Additional Suggestions* provided in the **Teacher's Guide** at the end of each unit offer activities that can help you accomplish this.

SUGGESTED TIMES

Each section of the *Suggested Directions* in the **Teacher's Guide** includes approximate times for the activities within that section. These estimates will help you plan individual lessons or instructional periods. Unit time estimates range from about one to three hours. Our field test has demonstrated that 20 to 25 minutes of working with study skills is a productive amount of time. Thus you will need to plan for several blocks of time to complete the activities in each unit.

Our classroom testing experience has also shown us that wide variation in teaching style and student levels results in an equally wide variation in the instructional time needed for any one exercise. We suggest that you examine the **Program's** units carefully and gauge your planning of instructional time according to your knowledge of how things actually work in your classroom.

SUGGESTED DIRECTIONS

You will be able to teach each unit more effectively if you examine both its **Student Text** and **Teacher's Guide** versions in their entirety before you begin the unit. Then carefully read the *Suggested Directions*.

Our classroom testing of these directions has shown them to be effective. Of course, we invite you to adapt them in ways that are appropriate for your students.

In some cases the **Teacher's Guide** gives specific directions to be read aloud to students. However, usually you will need to put the instructions into your own words.

CREATIVE DRAMATICS ACTIVITIES

Several units include a creative dramatics activity. Creative dramatics is an extremely effective method of instruction for young children because it is an holistic and imaginative approach to learning. Keep the following in mind when leading these activities:

- Students' enthusiasm and energy level may be higher than for other activities.

- It may take several attempts before you and your students are familiar and comfortable with this method of instruction.

- Students will often enjoy repeating these activities.

- Creative dramatics may be effectively used as a method of instruction in any curriculum area.

A POTPOURRI OF HINTS AND SUGGESTIONS

USING SMALL GROUPS IN THE CLASSROOM

For some of the activities in the **hm Program,** we have recommended organizing your students into small working groups. We have done this for the following reasons:

(1) Small group processes genuinely engage students in an activity.

(2) Students can share their talents and experience and learn from each other.

(3) Because they offer active participation to each and every student, such processes help both to enhance motivation for learning and increase interest in the content of a lesson.

You may wish to select the membership of the small groups for each exercise based upon your knowledge of your students. Some teachers have found it valuable to maintain fixed groups for periods of time to offer students the experience of developing positive and efficient working relationships.

Individual work is also of critical importance to the learning of study skills. When a skill has been introduced in a group setting, it is necessary to provide for individual work with that skill through other activities.

STUDENT DISCUSSION

Students need the opportunity to discuss their work if they are to learn study skills effectively and know how and when to use them. Their discussion must include not only the "right answer" (if there is one) but also the process through which they arrived at the answer and their reasons for considering it correct. At this point in your students' development of study skills, *the process is more important than the individual answer.* For these reasons, we have included oral activities and the opportunity for small and large group discussion throughout the **Program**.

LEARNING STUDY SKILLS: LEARNING FROM ERRORS

An important key to teaching study skills is the recognition that learning a study skill requires most learners to err before they can succeed. We learn skills by being presented with a new skill, trying to use that skill ourselves, committing errors, identifying our errors and then correcting them. Understanding this process creates several responsibilities for the teacher:

(a) The teacher must encourage students to ask questions when they do not understand an idea or directive. Knowing when to ask questions is an important characteristic of the effective learner.

(b) The teacher must provide a space within the learning process where students can try out a new skill, make errors, but not feel that they have failed or are "failures."

(c) The teacher must provide students with enough opportunities for practice of the new skill so that students begin to master the skill and see its usefulness.

(d) The teacher must provide usable feedback to students about the effectiveness of their use of the new study skill so that they understand that they can now do certain things that they could not do before.

(e) The teacher must reward students for what they have done well in using the new study skill. With such recognition, students experience success in the learning process, validated both by their own new ability and by the teacher's recognition of this. The experience of success motivates students to continue the development of mastery of the new study skill.

STUDENT EVALUATIONS

You may want to give yourself and your students an opportunity to evaluate both individual activities and entire units. This can be accomplished through whole class discussion.

For evaluating individual activities, you might ask students questions such as these: Did you like this activity? Did it help you to observe (listen, visualize, etc.) better?

For evaluating and summarizing units, possible questions might be these: What activities did we do to learn about observing (listening, visualizing, etc.)? What did these activities teach you about observing?

ADDITIONAL SUGGESTIONS

Additional Suggestions for each unit are provided in the **Teacher's Guide.** These suggestions are ideas and activities that build on the skills and concepts introduced in the units. These suggestions provide opportunities for additional practice of the study skill(s) and demonstrate a variety of applications of each new skill. We recommend that you read through the *Additional Suggestions* prior to teaching a unit. This will give you a better sense of the purpose and direction of the unit.

We suggest that you plan to use some of the relevant suggested activities in the days following your teaching of each of the **Program's** units. You'll want to keep others in mind for use later in the year.

ADDITIONAL COMMENTS

The **hm Study Skills Program: Level A** is designed for use by a teacher in a classroom setting. It is not programmed material that students can work through by themselves.

The **hm Study Skills Program: Level A** incorporates student activity as much as possible, including individual, small group, and whole class activities. This emphasis on activity results from our conviction that people learn skills best by doing.

Some teachers have found the **hm Program** useful as a diagnostic tool. It can show you what your students' current level of competence is and where you need to focus your instructional attention.

We strongly recommend that you tell your students why you think study skills are important in the classroom and in life.

OTHER hm STUDY SKILLS PROGRAMS

The **hm Study Skills Program: Level A** for 1st and 2nd graders is the most recent addition to a series of study skills programs that includes the following:

The hm Study Skills Program: Level B .... for grades 3-4

The hm Study Skills Program: Level I (Revised) .... for grades 5-7

The hm Math Study Skills Program .... for grades 6-10

The hm Science Study Skills Program .... for grades 7-10

The hm Study Skills Program: Level II (Revised) .... for grades 8-10

The hm College Study Skills Program: Level III .... for grades 11-13

The hm GED Study Skills Program .... for those preparing for the GED Tests

UNIT 1
Listening

Introduction

The ability to listen effectively is critical for success in school as well as for maximizing learning potential. Students come to school with a variety of abilities in listening skills. We can teach students to become more skilled and thus more effective listeners. The activities in this unit are aimed toward that goal.

Effective listening skills include both the ability to hear a wide range of sounds in the environment and the ability to listen selectively to the specific sounds needed for a particular learning activity, such as listening to the teacher's instruction, listening to a classmate's feedback, or listening to a record.

Approximate Time for Unit 1: 90 TO 130 MINUTES

You'll want to teach this unit and all of the units in more than one session, with periods of no more than 30 to 35 minutes.

There are many possible ways of scheduling this unit. You might teach it in daily periods during one week. You could teach Activities #1 and #2 on one day; #3 on the next day; #4 and #5 on the next; #6 and #7 on the following day; and #8 on the fifth. You may want to include ADDITIONAL ACTIVITIES at other times during the day or use them to extend the unit into the following week.

If you choose to teach this unit in shorter periods of time, you could present fewer activities on each day and extend the time spent on this unit to two weeks.

UNIT **1**

Listening

Introduction

This is a picture of an ear.

You hear with your ears.
Hearing is something you do all the time, without thinking about it.

You also listen with your ears.
Listening is a kind of hearing.
Listening is careful hearing.
Listening happens when you think about what you hear.

Your teacher will give you some activities to help you listen well.

SUGGESTED ACTIVITIES FOR UNIT 1
ACTIVITY ONE: What Does "Listening" Mean?

Hand out the **Study Skills Program** to your students. Ask your students to turn to page 1. Read aloud and discuss the *Introduction*. Make sure that your students understand the difference between hearing and listening. Stress that listening requires a special effort.

Discuss the picture on the bottom of the page. Ask which students look as if they are listening to the teacher. Say that you will be doing some activities and games to help your students become better listeners.

Approximate Time: 5 TO 10 MINUTES

ACTIVITY TWO: Listening to Sounds around Us

Tell your students that everyone will close her/his eyes and be completely quiet for one minute, listening to all of the sounds in the environment. Explain that after the minute is over, they will have an opportunity to name the sounds they have heard.

Ask your students to close their eyes and begin to listen. When the minute is over, ask your students to name sounds that they heard while you write the words on the blackboard. Praise students for listening well to hear many sounds.

Approximate Time: 5 TO 10 MINUTES

ACTIVITY THREE: Secret Sounds

Tell your students that you will be making some "secret sounds." They will need to close their eyes and listen very carefully so they can name the object that is making each sound. Make some of the following sounds, one at a time, preferably behind your desk or a screen. After each sound, stop and have your students open their eyes and tell what they think made the sound. Then demonstrate so that they can see sound being made.

a. you whistle

b. play musical instrument(s) that the students are familiar with, such as bell, tambourine, triangle, drum, cymbal, recorder. (If you have a variety of them, use one at a time.)

c. crumple piece of paper

d. write on paper with pencil

e. clap hands

f. write with chalk on board

g. breathe loudly

h. tap shoes on floor

i. make any other common sounds in your classroom

You may want to allow students to think of other sounds and take turns going behind your desk or screen to make their sound for others to guess.

Approximate Time: 10 TO 15 MINUTES

ACTIVITY FOUR: Team Telephone

Set up the chairs or desks in two or three parallel lines of ten to fifteen desks, with all of the desks or chairs facing the front of the classroom. Be sure that there is at least ten feet between lines. Have students sit in each line facing the front. Each line is a team.

Tell students that you are going to play "telephone." Explain the following: Each team is a telephone line. You will whisper the same short message to the student at the front of each line. Each telephone line will pass this whispered message from front to back, with the first person turning around and whispering the message to the second person, the second person passing it to the third person, etc. The goal is for the message to be passed correctly to the last person in the line. Each team receives a point for each correctly transmitted message. (If you would prefer a noncompetitive game, you may omit keeping score.) Be sure that students understand that it is accuracy, not speed, that is being rewarded in this game.

Whisper a two or three word message to the first person in each line. Allow students to pass on the message as soon as they hear it. After the message has reached the last person in each line, ask each last student to say it aloud. You announce or ask one of the first students to announce the initial message. Give a point to each team that has passed the message correctly from front to back, if you are using points.

After each message, have the students on each team move up one seat and have the first person move to the back, allowing each student a turn to begin a message. After students understand the game, the teacher may allow students to invent their own messages. Continue until each student has had a turn to start the message.

You may announce the winner of the game if you are playing competitively. In either case, praise all students for their careful listening skills.

Approximate Time: 15 TO 20 MINUTES

ACTIVITY FIVE: Changing the Circles

Give each student a pencil or crayon. Ask your students to turn to page 2 of the **Study Skills Program.** Ask them what they see on the page. Wait until they have indicated that they see circles of different sizes. Tell them to listen carefully to you.

Explain that you will ask them to change each circle into a different picture with their pencil or crayons. Note that they can use their pencil or crayons to add anything they want to the circles and they will have to listen well to find out how to change each circle.

Read the following directions aloud, one at a time. Say **"Change the biggest circle into a SUN."** Allow time for students to do this. **"Change the next biggest circle into a FACE with eyes, a nose, a mouth, and anything else you want to put on it."** Allow drawing time. **"Change the next biggest circle into an ANIMAL, any kind of animal that you want."** Allow drawing time. **"Change the last two little circles into a CAR, using the little circles for wheels."** Allow drawing time.

Now ask your students to divide into pairs or other size groupings to show their pictures to each other. Have them explain to each other what they drew and talk about any difficulties they had in doing this activity.

Approximate Time: 10 TO 15 MINUTES

ACTIVITY SIX: Listening in a Discussion

Have a group discussion about circuses. Give the following directions: **"Now each person who wishes can tell one thing about a circus. You can raise your hand, and I will call on you. But there is one special rule: you must listen very carefully to what each person says. To show that you are listening, you must repeat what the person before you said before you can say something. If I say: 'I love to eat peanuts at the circus,' you can say: 'Ms. . . . . . likes to eat peanuts when she goes to the circus.' You don't have to repeat exactly what is said, but you must be close. You can shorten it if the person uses lots of words. Then you can say something else about circuses. Now I will start..."**

Begin with an appropriate comment. Then allow each student a turn. Stop students from making more than one comment. Help students who are having difficulty repeating what has been said.

Approximate Time: 15 TO 20 MINUTES

ACTIVITY SEVEN: Sound Effects for a Story

Give the following directions to the students: **"I am going to read you a story about a circus. When you hear me say certain special words in the story, I want you to make special sounds that I will teach you now. Right after you make the special sound, you will need to be quiet so you can hear the next special word. When you hear me say LION, I want you to ROAR like a lion. Try it now...When you hear me say LION TAMER, I want you to CLAP as if you're cracking a whip. Try it now...When you hear me say HORSES, I want you to SLAP your thighs, as if you are horses galloping. Try it now...When you hear me say CLOWNS, I want you to laugh. Try it now...When you hear me say PEOPLE, I want you to cheer. Try it now...When you hear me say BANG, I want you to yell 'BANG' all together, just one time. Try it now..."**

"Now we're ready to begin the story. If you make the special sounds when you hear the word, I'll know you are listening. Remember to be quiet right after you have made the sound so you can hear the rest of the story."

Read the story slowly, pausing after each word in capital letters.

The Circus Accident

The big three-ring circus was about to begin. The **PEOPLE** in the audience were excited. The **LIONS** were pawing restlessly, waiting for their act. The **LION TAMER** was waiting, too. The **HORSES** were lined up outside the bigtop, waiting to enter. The **CLOWNS** were practicing their silly tricks. Suddenly there was a loud **BANG.** The cannon from the human cannonball act had gone off ahead of time by accident. Everything went wild. The **LION TAMER** ran off to see what had happened, forgetting that he had left the **LION'S** cage open. The **LIONS** ran off into the ring. The **HORSES** were afraid of the loud noise, and they ran wildly into the ring, too, going round and round in circles. The **LION TAMER** ran after the **LIONS,** and the **CLOWNS** ran after the **HORSES.** The **PEOPLE** cheered. They thought it was part of the show. The **LION TAMER** caught up with the **LIONS** and got them back into their cages. The **CLOWNS** jumped on the **HORSES'** backs and slowed them down. Now the real circus acts were ready to begin, but the **PEOPLE** thought they had already seen the best act.

Praise the students for listening well. Now tell them that you will read the story again and that you want them to show you that they can listen even better this time. Explain that they will show you this by making each special sound right after they hear each special word and then becoming quiet to hear the next special word.

Approximate Time: 10 TO 15 MINUTES

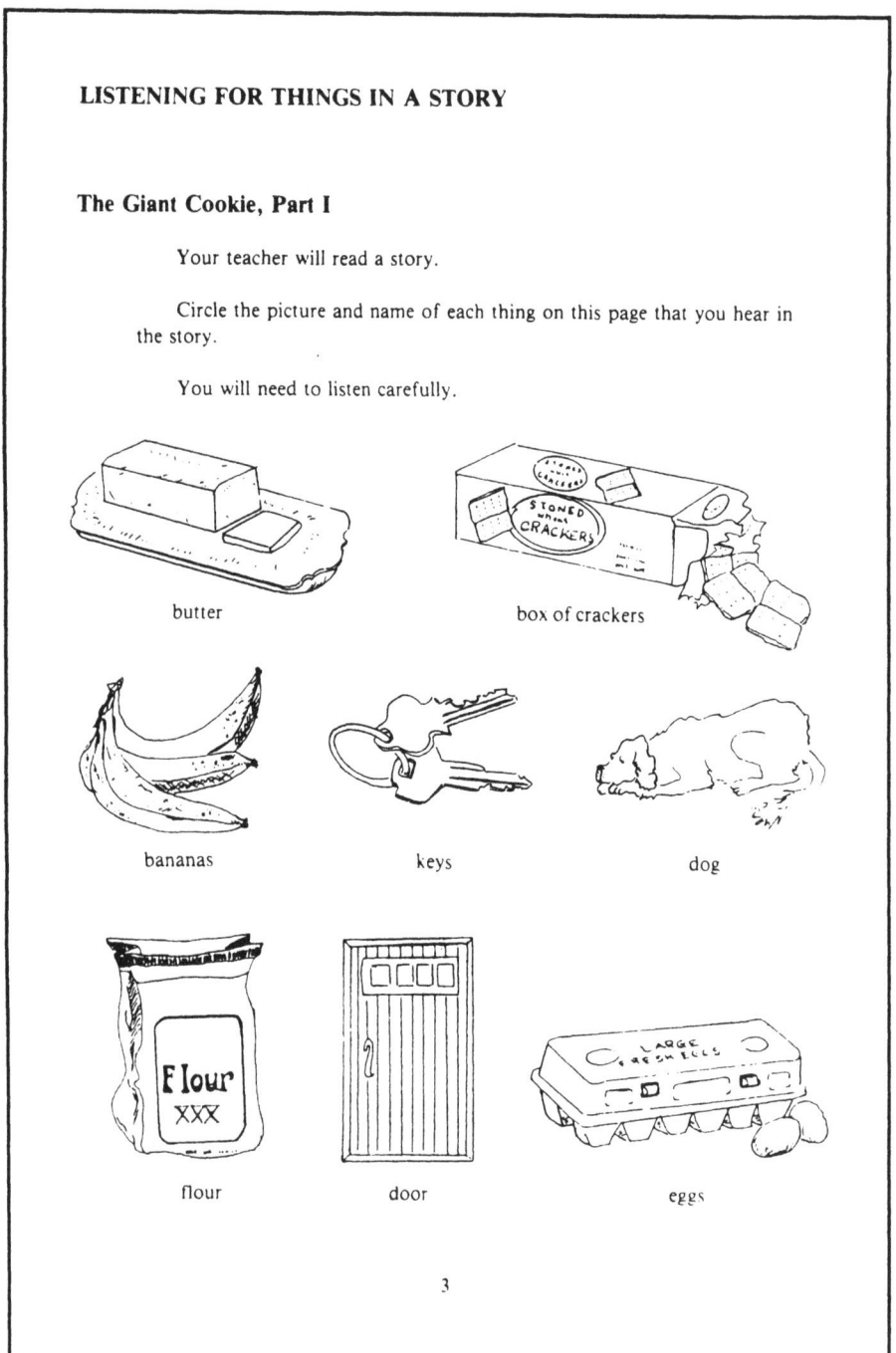

ACTIVITY EIGHT: Listening for Things in a Story

Give each student a crayon or pencil. Ask your students to open up their books to page 3. Tell your students to notice the pictures on the page. Have them take turns naming all the objects in the pictures. Then read the directions on the page aloud. Tell your students that you are going to read aloud the story *The Giant Cookie, Part 1*. Ask them to listen very carefully and to circle the picture of each thing that they hear named in the story. Tell them that the pictures on the page will not all be named in the story. Read the story slowly, slightly emphasizing each capitalized word.

The Giant Cookie, Part I

Sonya and Mark lived next to each other and walked home from school together each afternoon. Sonya often went to Mark's house to play until her mother and father came home from work. That is what she was doing one Wednesday afternoon in October. Sonya and Mark opened the **DOOR** to Mark's house and closed it loudly behind them. Mark's Dad came running to greet them, and so did Mark's **DOG**, Daisy. "Hi, kids," Mark's Dad said. "I have to finish writing a story. I'll be in my office for about half an hour. Help yourself to milk and **CRACKERS** for snack.

Sonya and Mark went to the kitchen. "I don't want crackers, I want cookies," Mark said. "Do you have any cookies?" asked Sonya. "No, but we can make them," answered Mark. "Do you know how to make cookies?" Sonya asked, looking at Mark in surprise. "Sure, I've seen my Dad do it lots of times," he answered.

Mark got out a large bowl. He put in two sticks of **BUTTER** and mashed them up. Then he asked Sonya to crack two **EGGS** in a smaller bowl and beat them up. Next he asked her to dump the beaten eggs in the big bowl and mix them with the butter while he put in some sugar and **FLOUR**. "How do you know how much to put in?" asked Sonya. "I know from watching my Dad," he answered. "OK, if you say so," Sonya said, but she didn't look too sure. After everything was mixed together, Sonya asked, "Isn't this dough a little too soft and mushy?" "It gets hard when you bake it," said Mark.

Now stop and ask the students which pictures they circled. Clarify that all pictures except those of the keys and the banana should be circled. Ask if the students had any problems in listening and circling the pictures.

Tell your students to turn to page 4. Ask them to name the pictures on that page. Say that you will read aloud *The Giant Cookie, Part 2*. Ask them to circle the pictures of the objects that they hear, just as they did last time. Note that in the first part of the story you read the names of the things in the pictures a little louder to help them. Explain that this time you won't do that so that they will need to listen VERY carefully. Then read the story slowly.

The Giant Cookie, Part 2

Sonya and Mark each took two **spoons** and made small, round cookies all over the cookie sheet. When they were done, Mark's Dad walked into the kitchen. "We made cookies," Mark announced, "and you're just in time to turn on the **oven** for us." Mark's Dad looked surprised, but he just said, "What busy kids!" Then he turned on the oven. Mark and Sonya put in the cookie sheets, set the timer, and waited for the cookies to be done. When the timer went off, they were excited. "I can hardly wait to taste these cookies," Sonya said. Mark carefully opened the hot oven door — and then he screamed. "Help! The giant cookie has taken over!" Sonya's eyes seemed to grow bigger as she stared at the cookie sheet. All the little cookies had melted into one, and that one cookie now filled the whole sheet.

Mark's father came running. He started to laugh when he saw the giant cookie. "I guess you put in a little too much butter and not quite enough flour," he said. "But after it cools a few minutes, we can break it into small pieces, and it will probably taste great."

Mark and Sonya laughed and laughed as they poured themselves two big **glasses** of **milk.** "I thought you knew how to make cookies," Sonya said. "Well, I almost did," Mark answered. "I did know how to make one cookie." Then they sat on two **chairs** and ate the crisp and delicious pieces of cookie.

Ask students which pictures they circled. Clarify that all except those of forks, carrots, and bread should be circled.

Now lead a discussion about the story. Ask students to explain why Mark and Sonya made one giant cookie instead of many smaller ones. Ask if they or their parents have ever tried to cook something that turned out different from what they expected.

Approximate Time: 20 TO 25 MINUTES

LISTENING FOR THINGS IN A STORY

The Giant Cookie, Part 2

Your teacher will read a story.

Circle the picture and name of each thing on this page that you hear in the story.

You will need to listen carefully.

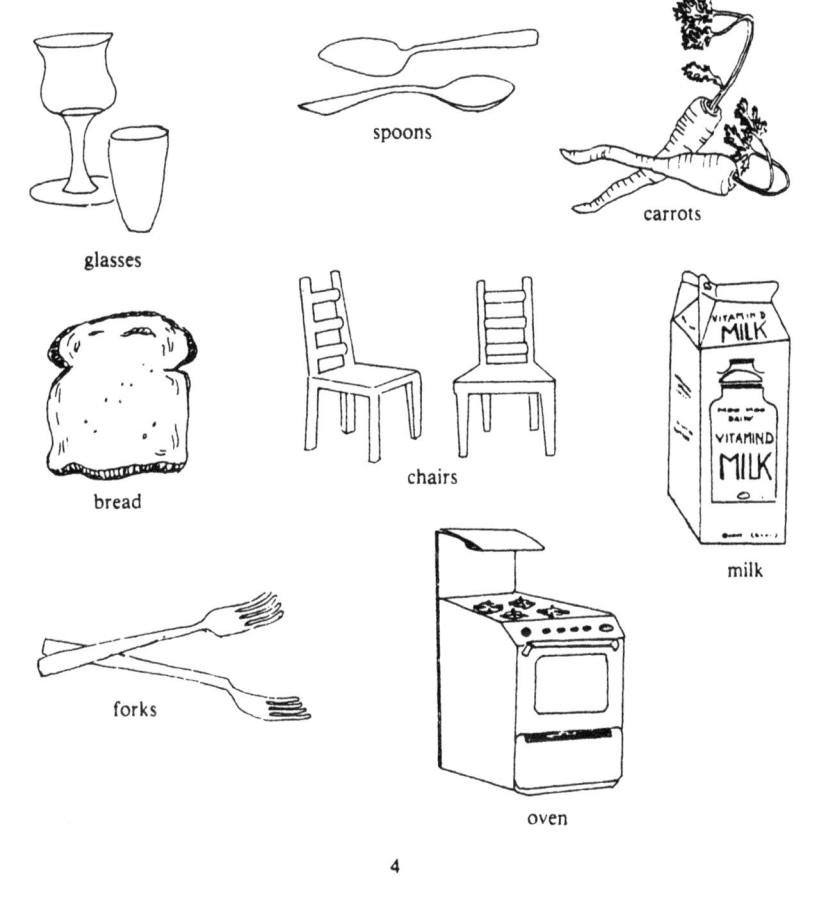

ADDITIONAL ACTIVITIES FOR UNIT 1

NAME GAME

Ask each student to sing his or her name in a different tune and rhythm. Have the whole group listen and sing it back in the same way. You might want to sing some examples first.

TAPE RECORDER

Use a tape recorder to record common household and school sounds, such as footsteps, chalk on blackboard, water running, a doorbell ringing, a door opening and shutting, a vacuum cleaner, and a broom sweeping. Play the sounds to the students, one at a time, and have them guess what they are hearing.

MAKE A NOISE

Ask each student, one at a time, to get up and make a noise with one or two objects in the classroom. For example, a student could hit an eraser against a chalkboard or close a book loudly. Each student must think of a new sound.

LISTENING TO SOUNDS AROUND US OUTDOORS

Take your students outdoors to a place where they can sit down. Ask them to close their eyes and listen to all of the sounds around them, as in Activity Two. After a minute, ask them to open their eyes and take turns naming the sounds that they heard.

SOUND CENTER

Make a sound center by putting an assortment of materials on a table. Allow your students to take turns improvising sounds in the sound center. Materials might include hub caps, sandpaper, shells, tin pans, cardboard tubes, cans, straws, spoons, pans, bells, combs, eggbeaters, tissue paper and/or cotton balls. Include a set of musical instruments, if you have them.

SOUND COLLECTING WALK

Go on a walk with a tape recorder. Try to collect as many sounds as possible. Play them back in the classroom, and identify them.

SOUND SYMPHONIES

Guide your students to find all of the different vocal sounds they can make. Then divide up into groups of four or five. Have each group decide on a different sound. Choose a conductor, and produce a "sound symphony."

HIGH AND LOW, SOFT AND LOUD

Use a piano or other musical instrument to teach the concepts "high" and "low," "soft" and "loud." Let the students label sounds from these categories. For example, play a low, soft note, and have students label it; then play a high, loud one, etc.

NAME THAT VOICE

Record each student talking on a tape recorder, without saying names. Have each student say the same sentence or two. Play back the recording, and have your students identify each other by the sound of their voices.

STETHOSCOPE

Borrow a real stethoscope. Let the students listen to their own or each other's heartbeats.

POPCORN

Make popcorn for snack with a hot air popper. Ask your students to listen carefully for the sound of the first kernel popping. Use a clock to time the popping. Also listen carefully for sound of the last kernel popping.

FREEZE AND MOVE

Use a lively record or tape-recorded piece of music. Explain to your students that they must listen very carefully for the music to stop. As soon as it stops, they must freeze. Explain that freezing means stopping completely in the position you are caught in and not moving anything, even your mouth. They must stay frozen until the music starts again. Now begin to play the music, and stop it suddenly. Make sure the students have "frozen" before you go on. Repeat a number of times.

MAGIC WORD

Select a "magic word" for the day. Instruct your students to listen for this word all day. Each time they hear you use this word, they should raise their hands. The word should be a commonly used one, such as "time" or "book."

SIMON SAYS

Play *Simon Says*. Have your students stand with some space around them. Explain that you will tell them actions to make with their bodies, but they should only do those things if you say "Simon Says" first. So they must listen very carefully. For example, if you say "Simon says 'raise your arms,'" the students should raise their arms. But if you say "Jump up and down," they shouldn't do it because Simon didn't tell them. The students can take turns being "Simon."

GROUP STORY

Tell the students that the whole class will write a story together. Say that you will start the story with one sentence, and each person will add a sentence. Stress that each student must listen very carefully so that the whole story will make sense. Be ready to write the story on the blackboard or on a large tablet as it is told. Read the whole story back to the class when it is done.

TAPE RECORDED STORIES

Have a number of different tape recorded stories available to the students to listen to when they have finished other work. You could suggest that they draw a picture to illustrate each story that they hear.

UNIT **2**

Observing

Introduction

Students need to attend to a situation or task before they can process the information and store it for later retrieval and use. Attention skills require students to notice (see) and examine (look closely). Both elements are necessary if students are to learn. When both elements are enacted, we call this *observing*.

This unit is designed to help students increase their observation skills through training and practice. The activities in the unit make explicit what we do every day so we can learn. These activities will enhance the students' abilities to see information and examine it closely.

Approximate Time for Unit 2: 80 TO 125 MINUTES

You'll want to teach this unit in more than one session with periods of no more than 30-35 minutes each.

There are many possible ways of scheduling this unit. You might teach it in daily periods during one week. You could teach Activities #1, #2, and #3 on one day; activities #4, #5, and #6 on the next; activities #7 and #8 on the following day; and activity #9 on the next. On the fifth day you might choose from ADDITIONAL ACTIVITIES at the end of the unit. You may want to include ADDITIONAL ACTIVITIES at other times during the day or use them to extend the unit to the following week.

SUGGESTED ACTIVITIES FOR UNIT 2

ACTIVITY ONE: Introduction

Ask your students to open their **Programs** to page 5. Ask them to look at the picture. Allow them 30 seconds to do so. Then have them shut their **Programs.**

Ask your students to raise their hands to indicate if they saw (a) a duck or (b) a rabbit.

Now have your students open their books to page 6. Ask them to follow along while you read the *Introduction.*

Introduction

If you look carefully at the picture on page 5, you can see two animals, a duck and a rabbit.

When you look carefully at something, we call it **observing**.

6

Have your students turn to page 5 again. Help them observe the picture. Show them both sides of the optical illusion. Cover up the left side of the picture with a blank piece of paper. Point out the rabbit's eye and mouth. Gradually slide the blank page to the left allowing the ears of the rabbit to appear. Make certain that all students perceive the rabbit before proceeding. Next cover up the right side of the picture with a blank page. Point out the duck's beak. Gradually slide the blank paper to the right, allowing the students to see the duck's eye. Make certain that all students perceive the duck before proceeding.

Talk to students about how things may not always be only what they seem at first glance. Explain the necessity of examining some things closely so you can see all the parts. Also talk about how things may appear to be different to different people.

Approximate Time: 10 TO 15 MINUTES

ACTIVITY TWO: What Did You See?

Instruct your students to close their eyes and try to recall the details of the room. Then ask questions like the ones listed below. After each question ask your students to raise their hands if they think the description is accurate or true. Take a quick count of the number of students who give yes and no answers. Have students open their eyes and check their answers. Ask leading questions such as the ones below. Be sure that some of the descriptions are not accurate.

Are there five groups of desks?

Are there three plants?

Is there writing on the blackboard?

Does the bulletin board have pictures of fall leaves?

When you have asked all of the questions, talk with your students about how their answers may have been more accurate if they had carefully examined the room before they had been asked to close their eyes.

Ask your students to observe the room carefully. Give them time to do so; then repeat the exercise above, using questions with more detail.

After the activity, talk with your students about how observing involves looking closely at something.

Approximate Time: 10 TO 15 MINUTES

ACTIVITY THREE: Notice Me

For this activity you will need to stand behind a screen or crouch behind your desk. Tell your students that you are going to ask them some questions. Have your students close their eyes. Ask them questions about your appearance, such as the following ones:

Am I wearing a red dress?

Am I wearing jewelry?

Am I wearing white socks?

Ask the students to raise their hands if they think the answer is "Yes." Take a quick count of the number of yes and no answers. When you have asked all of the questions, have your students open their eyes and observe you carefully to see how well they answered the questions.

Then organize your students into pairs. Have students observe each other's appearance. Instruct them to look at the color of clothing their partner is wearing, hair color and length, color of eyes, kind of sneakers, and so on. Then have one student in each pair close his/her eyes. Have the other student in each pair ask questions about his/her appearance such as the following:

What color clothes do I have on?

What color are my eyes?

What color is my hair?

Do I have something in my hair?

Does my shirt have stripes on it?

Am I wearing sneakers?

Encourage your students to ask additional questions if they want. When the time is up, have the students whose eyes are closed open their eyes. Encourage both students in each pair to share their observations about each other's behavior. You can direct this part of the activity by asking what kinds of things they observed: dress colors, types of shoes, hair and eye color, and so on.

Repeat the activity with the partners switching roles. At the end of a time, ask the students to share their observations.

Approximate Time: 10 TO 15 MINUTES

ACTIVITY FOUR: Changes

As a follow-up to the preceding exercise, ask the partners to observe each other simultaneously. Tell them that you will ask them to turn away and make two changes to their appearance. For example, one student may unbutton her/his shirt; another may turn a collar in. Ask the students to give you other examples to make sure they understand. Then have them turn away and make the changes. Have them turn back and see if their partners notice. If the partners do not identify the changes, have their partners tell them.

Approximate Time: 5 TO 10 MINUTES

ACTIVITY FIVE: Mirroring

Organize your students into pairs. Designate one student in each pair as the *leader*. Ask the *leaders* to begin to move parts of their body. Ask the other students to copy or mirror the performance of their partner. Instruct the *leaders* to move very slowly and the *mirrorers* to do exactly as their partner does, as if both students were looking in a mirror. Have the students stay in place as they do this activity. After two minutes repeat the activity with students switching roles.

Then talk with your students about the difficulties of observing movement.

Approximate Time: 5 TO 10 MINUTES

HOCUS FOCUS

Look at the two pictures.

Compare the pictures by looking at them closely.

Circle the things in picture A that are different from the things in picture B.

Picture A

Picture B

ACTIVITY SIX: Hocus Focus

Instruct your students to look at the two pictures on page 7. Ask them to circle the things in picture A that are different from the things in picture B. Emphasize that they need to do a careful comparison, observing all the parts before they make a decision.

When the students have finished, go over the answers by having them discuss the parts they circled. Have them explain the differences they observed.

Approximate Time: 5 TO 10 MINUTES

DISAPPEARING PICTURE (A)

Look at the pictures on the next page.

Name all the things you see.

Some things seem to go together.

Name or write the groups that go together.

ACTIVITY SEVEN: Disappearing Picture

Tell your students to open their **Programs** to page 8. Read the page aloud. Then ask them to look at the display of things on page 9. Talk to them about what each thing is. Talk about associations between things, showing them how to make connections. For example, the shoe, dress, and blouse could go together because they are all things you can wear. Or the refrigerator, forks, spoons, and cup could go together because they all can be found in the kitchen. Encourage students to make their own associations while you write them on the board.

Now have students turn the page. Explain that they cannot turn back to the previous page. Ask them to look at the pictures and try to pick out what is missing. Have them draw a picture of the missing items.

When the students have finished, review the pictures. Compare them to the previous page. Remind the students that they need to look closely and remember what they observe by making connections between things.

Approximate Time: 10 TO 15 MINUTES

DISAPPEARING PICTURE (B)

Look at these pictures.

Can you tell what is missing?

Draw a picture of the things that are missing.

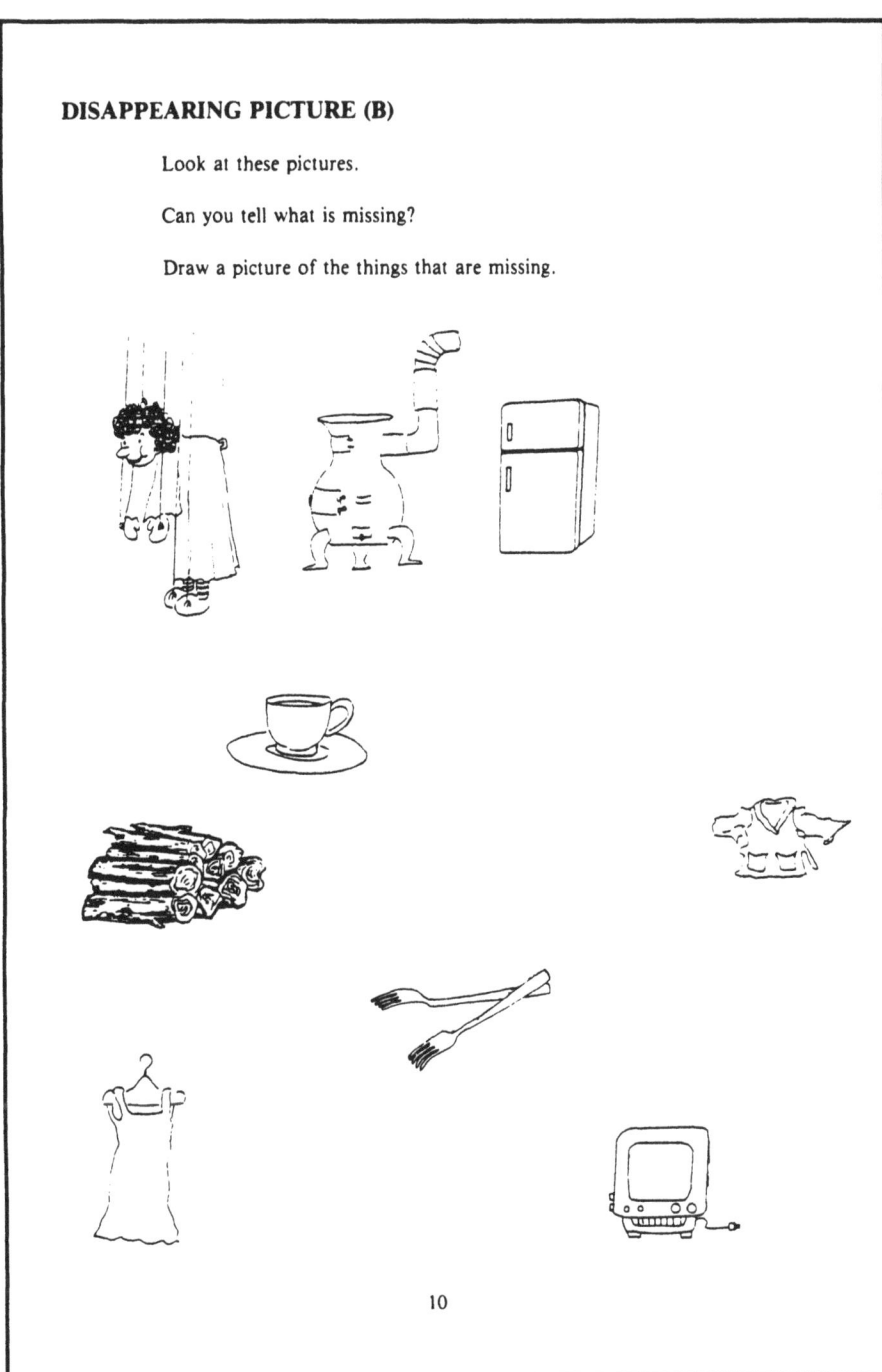

LET'S MAKE A STORY

Look carefully at this picture.

11

ACTIVITY EIGHT: Let's Make a Story

Have your students look at the picture on page 11. Tell them that they will be asked to observe what is happening. Remind them that *observe* means to look carefully and think about what they are looking at.

Engage your students in discussing the picture from the following perspectives:

What has already happened?

What is happening now?

Then ask your students to draw a picture of what might happen next on page 12. When they have finished, have them share their pictures with the class. Ask each student to describe her/his picture briefly.

Approximate Time: 15 TO 20 MINUTES

What will happen next?

12

ACTIVITY NINE: Improvised Action through Drama

Divide the class into groups of four or five students. Instruct each group to decide upon an activity they enjoy, such as swimming in the lake, building a snowman, making cookies, planting a garden, getting dressed for school, or playing baseball. If appropriate, you can limit the activities to the season, such as winter activities or spring activities.

Encourage your students to recall visual images of their chosen activity, including materials and objects. Ask them to think about the sizes of the objects and how they would use them.

After five minutes, have each group act out its activity. Give each group approximately two minutes to perform its actions. Have the rest of the class guess the activity. Guide the guessing by asking questions like the following ones:

   a. What activity did the players cause you to see?

   b. Where were the players?

   c. What objects did they use?

Approximate Time: 10 TO 15 MINUTES

ADDITIONAL ACTIVITIES FOR UNIT 2

MOVING WATER

Obtain a leafy celery stalk, and cut off about one inch from the bottom of it. Fill a glass shorter than the cut stalk half full of water. Add food coloring (combine red and blue) so the water is very dark.

Put the celery into the glass of dyed water, and set it under a bright light. Have the students check the celery every thirty minutes. The leaves will change color.

You can use a knife to remove the outer layer of the stalk. Students will be able to observe the colored lines running through it and see that this is part of the plant's drinking system.

PANTOMIME QUIZ

Using sounds but not words, pantomime a situation. For example: the teacher is reading; there is a knock at the door; the teacher goes to the door, but no one is there; this happens several times; finally, the teacher waits just behind the door; when the knock is heard again, the teacher quickly opens the door and surprises someone.

Ask the students to describe what happened after they have observed the pantomime. Then, in small groups, have them pantomime other situations using sounds.

BLOW, WIND, BLOW

Have each student or group of students make a weather vane.

Instruct the students to place a straight pin through the center of a drinking straw. Place a feather in one end of the straw, or slit the straw and insert an arrowhead made from cardboard.

Students should push the pin into the eraser of a pencil and then tie the pencil onto the end of a long stick or piece of wood.

By placing the stick in the ground, students will be able to observe and discuss the changing directions of the wind.

WEATHER, WEATHER

Make a calendar for the month.

Generate, with the class, various symbols for different kinds of weather.

Draw or mimeograph the agreed-upon symbols, and glue them on cardboard so that students can paste or hook them on the calendar.

Allow time during the day when students can observe the weather for the day and attach a symbol on the calendar that represents the weather for that day.

SEED CYCLE

Provide enough oranges and grapefruits for each student to have at least one section to eat. Gather the seeds, and place them in a shallow bowl.

Cover the seeds with water, and allow them to soak overnight.

Two days later have the students plant the seeds in paper cups by placing some soil in the bottom of each cup, placing three or four seeds on the soil, and then completely covering the seeds with more soil.

Place the paper cups on a sunny window sill, and keep the soil moist. It may take some time for the plants to begin to grow, but the sprouting will be interesting.

Make a large class chart to record the plants' growth, or have ditto sheets for the students to keep individual records of the growth. Showing and discussing pictures of grapefruit and orange trees in various stages of development will help develop the students' observation skills as they see changes from a seed to a plant.

OBSERVING WITH THINGS

Place eyeglasses, binoculars, a microscope, magnifying glasses, a kaleidoscope, and View Masters on a table.

Encourage your students to talk about the different ways these things are used for seeing.

Look at objects through a magnifying glass and a microscope.

Provide a tray of things for students to observe such as rocks, shells, and seeds. Also encourage them to observe objects in your room.

Engage your students in talking about what they are observing.

OBSERVATION WALK

Go for an observation walk. This can be a general or a specific walk, such as "Look for bugs" or "Look for leaves." Take some binoculars, a magnifying glass, and a sack for the treasures you may find.

Put large lengths of paper on the wall or the floor, and let the students paint or color what they saw on the walk.

BEFORE AND AFTER

Use cooking activities to engage your students in observing the difference in appearance of foods before and after cooking.

Suggested foods are: jello, gingerbread, pancakes, pudding, scrambled eggs, and popcorn.

OBSERVATION TABLE

Instruct your students to observe carefully as they walk around the school and their neighborhood. Ask them to look for interesting objects such as feathers, rocks, flowers, and leaves. Have a table for the students to bring their special finds for the week.

Have students observe each other's treasures.

Talk to students about where they found their treasure and what it is.

ANIMAL OBSERVATION

Purchase for the classroom a small animal pet (gerbil, guinea pig, turtle) to be observed by the students. Encourage children to describe what they discover by observing.

Create a chart that shows the pet's movement, sleep patterns, and so on.

LOOK AND SEE

Use several objects of different colors or shapes, such as a pencil, a paper clip, a straw, a shoelace, colored paper, and so on. Place them on a tray. Have students describe them. Then remove the tray from the students' sight so that you can secretly remove an object. Take one object away, and then ask your students to identify which one is missing. Encourage students to talk about how they knew which was missing.

I SEE SOMETHING, WHAT DO YOU SEE?

Tell your students that you are going to play a game. You will start by being the leader. Choose something in the room to focus on. Describe it in one sentence; for example, it is round. Students must ask questions to which you can respond only yes or no, such as, is it yellow? Students must try to guess the object.

WHO'S MISSING?

Have students close their eyes. Quietly remove one student from the room. Can the rest guess who's missing?

MATCH THEM

There are many commercially made Lotto games that can be used to enhance observation skills. Teachers can also make their own that focus on a basic theme or unit.

RECESS PICTURES

Take photographs of your students during recess time each month. Take the pictures in the same place each time. At the end of the year put them into a book. Students can observe the changes that take place in themselves from month to month.

WHAT'S DIFFERENT?

Change your appearance, and see if your students notice. For example, you could wear two different earrings, two different shoes, eye shadow on one eye, and so on.

UNIT 3
Understanding Directions

Introduction

Children are asked daily to follow directions. These directives come in varying lengths and forms. Sometimes children are told to perform one limited task. Other times they are given multi-step commands that need to be performed in a given sequence.

As teachers, we must realize that students vary in their abilities to carry out these directions. We need to be sensitive to the varying levels of skill that our students have in comprehending and following directions, and direct tasks and activities accordingly. We must also help our students to increase their direction-following skills. The most effective way to do this is to start with the most basic and proceed to more difficult levels. The activities in this unit begin with single directions where students perform simple tasks. Subsequent activities involve multi-step instructions where students need to hold each step in their memories, order the parts, and comprehend the whole task before beginning.

These activities are designed so that if your students have difficulties at any stage, you can design additional activities using the same format.

To a great degree, following directions depends on the student's ability to listen and observe. This unit is a logical extension of the previous units because it utilizes and further develops the skills presented in the first two units. Remind your students to listen carefully, observe what you say and do, and then proceed to perform the activity.

Approximate Time for Unit 3: 50 TO 90 MINUTES

You will want to teach this unit in more than one session with periods of no more than 30-35 minutes each.

There are many possible ways of scheduling this unit. You might teach it in daily periods in one week. You could teach Activities #1, #2, and #3 on one day; activities #4 and #5 on the next; activities #6 and #7 on the following day; and activities #8 and #9 on the next. On the fifth day you might choose from the ADDITIONAL ACTIVITIES at the end of the unit. You may want to include ADDITIONAL ACTIVITIES at other times during the day or use them to extend this unit to the following week.

UNIT **3**

Understanding Directions

Introduction

You hear directions every day.

Your teacher may give you directions.

Your parents may give you directions.

You also read directions every day.

Books have directions.

Signs also give you directions.

You need to listen or observe carefully to follow directions.

Now your teacher will give you some activities that will help you learn more about following directions.

13

SUGGESTED ACTIVITIES FOR UNIT 3

ACTIVITY ONE: What Does Understanding Directions Mean?

Ask your students to turn to page 13. Read the *Introduction* aloud. Ask students to follow along in their **Program** (if they read).

As you read, ask students to give examples of the directions that teachers give, that parents give, and that they read in books or see on signs (if they are readers). Invite them to share their experiences.

Remind students that they will need to listen carefully or read carefully if they are to follow directions correctly. Students also should be reminded that they need to take their time and work as carefully as they can in the following activities.

Approximate Time: 5 TO 10 MINUTES

ACTIVITY TWO: Read and Do

Ask your students to turn to page 14. Read direction #1 to them, and have them follow this instruction.

As the students begin, be certain that they understand the direction word in this sentence. Allow time for your students to follow the direction. Then have a volunteer give the correct answer.

Follow the same procedure for directions #2 - #6.

Approximate Time: 10 MINUTES

3. Underline the first and the last student in the row.

4. Put a check mark on the last two animals in the row.

5. Cross out the third and the last apple.

6. Circle the second, fourth, and sixth triangle.

ACTIVITY THREE: Build the Picture

Instruct your students to turn to page 17. Talk about the picture. Ask them questions such as the following: What is the frog doing? Where is the monkey? Invite students to comment about what is happening in the picture so that they become familiar with all of its parts.

Then tell your students that they are going to add to the picture. Explain that they must listen carefully to the directions so they can build the picture.

Read the first direction aloud. Have your students follow this direction. Give them time to do so. Then do the same with the remaining directions.

Encourage your students to talk about the picture again. You may want to have them tell stories about the picture they have created.

Approximate Time: 10 TO 15 MINUTES

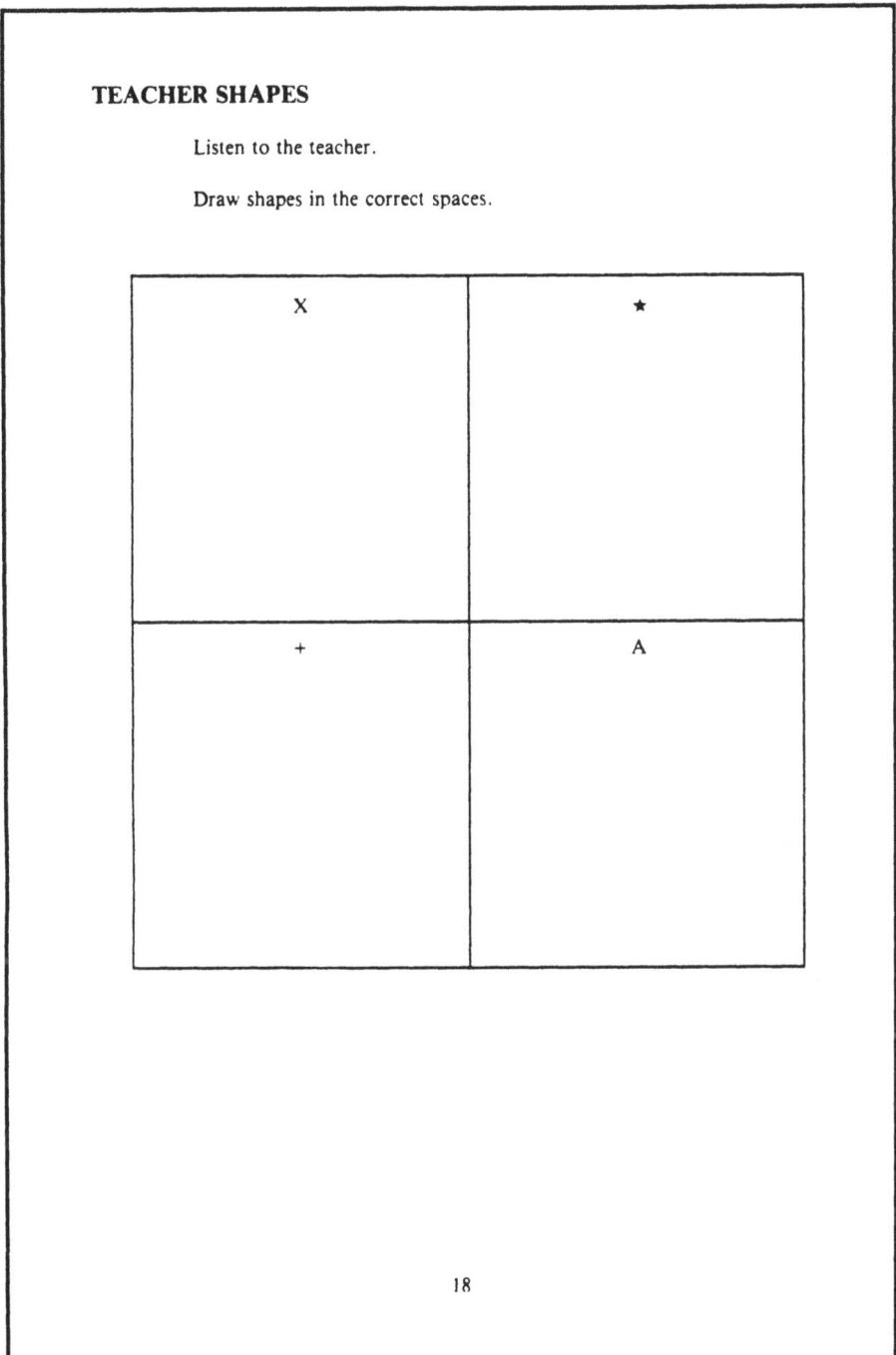

ACTIVITY FOUR: Teacher Shapes

Instruct the students to turn to page 18. Explain that this page is divided into four spaces. Then give direction #1. Once you have given the direction, make sure that each student can identify the correct space or quadrant. Then have your students follow the direction. Once they have done so, have a student show her/his circle to the group.

Follow the same procedure with directions #2 - #4.

1. Ask your students to point to the square with a ★ on it. Instruct them to draw a large circle in this space.

2. Ask your students to point to the square with a + on it. Instruct them to draw a square in this space.

3. Ask your students to point to the square with an X on it. Instruct them to draw a small circle in this space.

4. Ask your students to point to the square with the A on it. Instruct them to draw two little squares in this space.

Allow students time to color the shapes if they wish. You can also encourage them to make pictures of the shapes they have drawn.

Approximate Time: 5 TO 10 MINUTES

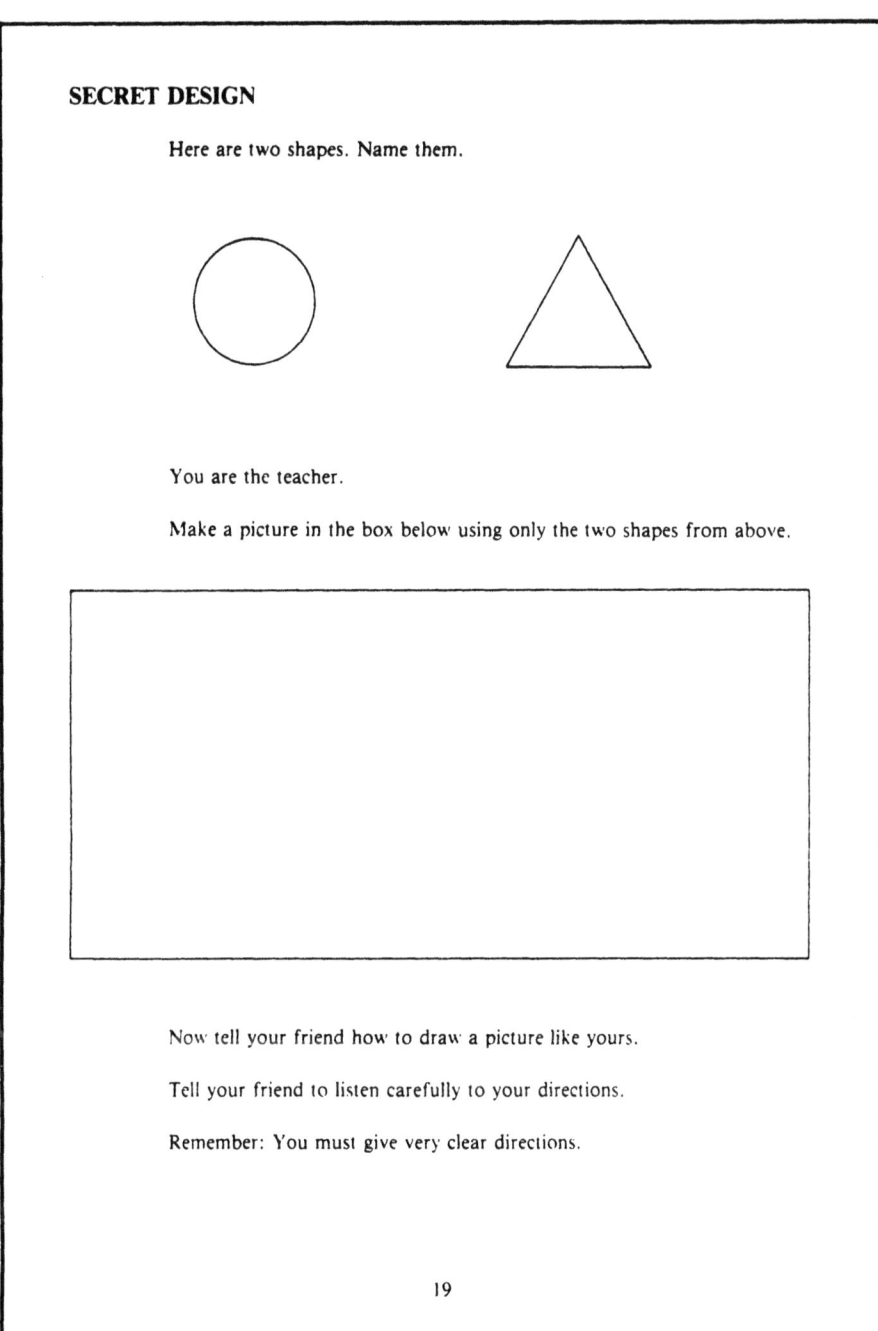

ACTIVITY FIVE: Secret Design

Ask your students to turn to page 19. Tell them that there are two shapes that they can use to create their own picture. Ask them to name the shapes: circle, triangle. Tell your students that you will give them two minutes to create a picture of their own using these two shapes in the space provided. Explain to them that they will have to be able to describe the picture they draw to a partner who will try to copy it from their directions. Note that their picture should be simple. Then ask them to begin.

This part of the activity may be difficult for some students so you may decide to do this part as a whole class activity. After a few minutes divide your students into pairs. Explain the following activity. Designate one student as the *drawer* and give him/her a blank sheet of paper. The other partner is the *teacher*. The teacher directs the drawer in drawing his/her picture.

Remind the students that the directions must be clear and simple. The *drawer* is not to look at the picture but may draw it only from the directions given by the *teacher*.

Hand out the sheets of paper, and have the pairs begin. Move around the room to give any help needed. When the drawers are finished, ask them to compare the completed designs with the original. Allow them time to talk about the differences and why the directions were or were not clear.

Then have your students change roles and repeat the activity.

When the task is completed, have the partners discuss the problems they had doing this activity. Then gather the class, and talk about how important it is to listen and observe carefully in order to follow directions. Also talk about how it is important to give clear directions so they can be heard and followed.

Approximate Time: 5 TO 10 MINUTES

DRAWING PICTURES FROM DIRECTIONS

In the box next to the sentence:

1. Draw a **house**.

   Draw a **window** in the **house**.

2. Draw a **circle**.

   Draw a **star** in the middle of the **circle**.

   Draw a **line** under the **circle**.

ACTIVITY SIX: Drawing Pictures from Directions

Ask your students to turn to page 20 in their **Program**. Read aloud the first set of directions. Then have your students draw the picture in the box as directed.

Follow the same procedure for #2.

Approximate Time: 5 TO 10 MINUTES

ACTIVITY SEVEN: My School

Draw a floor map of the school on the board, or use an overhead projector for this activity. Discuss with the whole class how to get to the following places in the school:

>   gym
>   lunch room
>   bathroom
>   music room
>   library

Have your students give you specific directions and step-by-step instructions for how to get to these places. Have your students describe how to get from one place to another.

Approximate Time: 10 TO 15 MINUTES

AROUND THE BARNYARD

On this page is a barnyard.

Listen to your teacher.

Find your way around the barnyard by listening to the directions.

21

ACTIVITY EIGHT: Around the Barnyard

Instruct your students to turn to page 21. Ask them to tell you about what they see. Tell students that you are going to give them directions for doing chores in the barnyard. Tell students that they must draw a path around the barnyard using the directions that you give them. Remind them that they must listen carefully and do the chores in the order you describe. Give the directions on the next page. As you give the first few directions, be sure that your students are drawing paths appropriately.

Begin by putting the tip of your pencil at the front door of the house.

Draw a path over the fence to pet the sheep.

Now climb over the fence to the barn door where you will find some oats, hay, and corn.

Feed the horse some of the oats.

Move down the path, over the farm machinery, and jump over the fence, which has fallen down.

Find the hole in the fence, and go under it to the pigs.

Feed the pigs.

While you are there, throw some corn to the chickens.

Crawl back through the hole in the fence to the cows.

You are tired from all your work, so find a corner where you can take a rest.

Draw yourself resting in the corner.

Approximate Time: 5 TO 10 MINUTES

ADDITIONAL ACTIVITIES FOR UNIT 3

OBSTACLE COURSE

Set up the room in an obstacle course. Have the students follow your verbal directions through the course. Then have the students give directions to other students.

FOLLOW MY LEAD

Give each student two paper clips, a red and a green piece of paper, and one crayon. Tell your students that you are going to give directions that they must follow. Give the following directions.

Part 1:

Place the crayon on the red paper.
Put the red paper on the green paper.
Put the crayon under the green paper.

Part 2:

Encourage your students to make something with the materials they have. Ask them to describe how they made it to a friend, giving step-by-step directions. If time permits, allow the friend to follow the instructions to make the design.

COOKING

Cooking is a natural activity for following directions since it involves listening, observing, and proceeding in step-by-step fashion. Pick a simple recipe such as one for peanut butter balls, and allow students to follow the directions given. For beginning readers, pictures can be used with words to make directions easier to follow.

UNIT 4
Categories

Introduction

A category is a group or class that can be used to sort things, information, and ideas. Categorization is one of the most basic of cognitive skills. We begin to use this skill in infancy, and we continue to use it all of our lives.

In schools we are constantly asking students to do tasks based on the ability to use categories in a variety of ways. Every subject we teach is based on a certain organization of information into categories. The kinds of categories used for reading, math, science, social studies, and so on are different, but students need to develop effective categorizing skills so that they can learn effectively in any of these areas.

This unit introduces the idea of categories and gives students practice in using and creating various types of categories.

Approximate Time for Unit 4: 105 TO 150 MINUTES

You'll want to teach this unit in more than one session, with periods of no more than 30 to 35 minutes.

There are many possible ways of scheduling this unit. You might teach it in daily periods during one week. You could teach Activities #1 and #2 on one day; #3 and #4 on the next day; #5 on the next day; #6, #7 and #8 on the following day; and #9 on the last day. You could use ADDITIONAL ACTIVITIES at other times during the day or use them to extend the unit into the following week.

If you choose to teach this unit in shorter periods, you could present fewer activities on each day and extend the time spent on this unit to two weeks.

PLEASE NOTE: Make a copy of pages 24-25 in the **Student Text** for each student prior to teaching this unit.

UNIT **4**

Categories

Introduction

A **category** is a name for a group of things that belong together in some way.

Cats, dogs, monkeys, cows, and elephants all belong to the category of animals.

What other things belong to the **category** of animals?

CATEGORY OF ANIMALS

The next activities you do will help you learn all about **categories**.

22

SUGGESTED ACTIVITIES FOR UNIT 4

ACTIVITY ONE: What Are Categories?

Ask your students to turn to page 22 in their **Programs.** Ask them to tell you what they see in the picture. Then read aloud the *Introduction.* After you read the question about "the category of animals," invite your students to give a number of answers. Write their answers on the board.

Approximate Time: 5 TO 10 MINUTES

ACTIVITY TWO: The Category of Things That Can Fly

Ask students to turn to page 23 of their **Study Skills Programs**. Ask them to name what they see in the picture. Wait until someone identifies the picture as clouds and sky. Affirm that this is a picture of the sky. Read aloud the title and directions on this page. Then say: **"I want you to draw pictures of all of the things you can think of that belong to the category of things that can fly."** Ask your students to begin drawing.

When the students have finished drawing, have them show and tell about what they drew. On the blackboard, list all of the things that your students drew, without repeating items. When you have completed the list, say something like the following: **"Each person thought of some things in the category of things that can fly. All of us together thought of all of these things. The category of things that can fly could be even bigger, because we might not have thought of everything."**

Approximate Time: 10 TO 15 MINUTES

ACTIVITY THREE: Thinking of Things in Categories

Tell the students that you are going to give them the name of a category and that you want them to name all of the things they can think of that belong in that category. Give each of the following categories, allowing time for students to think of many answers, about two or three minutes per category. Write student responses on the board. You may also want to include other categories that your students will enjoy exploring.

   a. Category of insects
   b. Category of desserts
   c. Category of things that are soft
   d. Category of things that grow in the ground
   e. Category of things made of wood

Approximate Time: 10 TO 15 MINUTES

ACTIVITY FOUR: Categories in the Classroom

Ask your students to look around the classroom and name things that belong in the category of things that are round. Encourage the students to name things until they can't think of any more.

Ask your students to look around the classroom and name things that belong in the category of things that are square.

Follow the same procedure for the following categories:

a. things that are larger than the teacher's chair

b. things that are smaller than children's hands

c. things that are black

d. things that can be read

e. things that work by electricity

Now hold up each of the following objects, and ask your students to name some categories into which the object could fit.

a. book (For example, a book belongs in the category of things with corners, the category of things that can be read, the category of things bigger than my hand, and the category of a particular color.)

b. pencil

c. paper

d. ruler

e. shoe

Now ask students to think of other categories that can be used to divide up things in the classroom.

Approximate Time: 15 TO 20 MINUTES

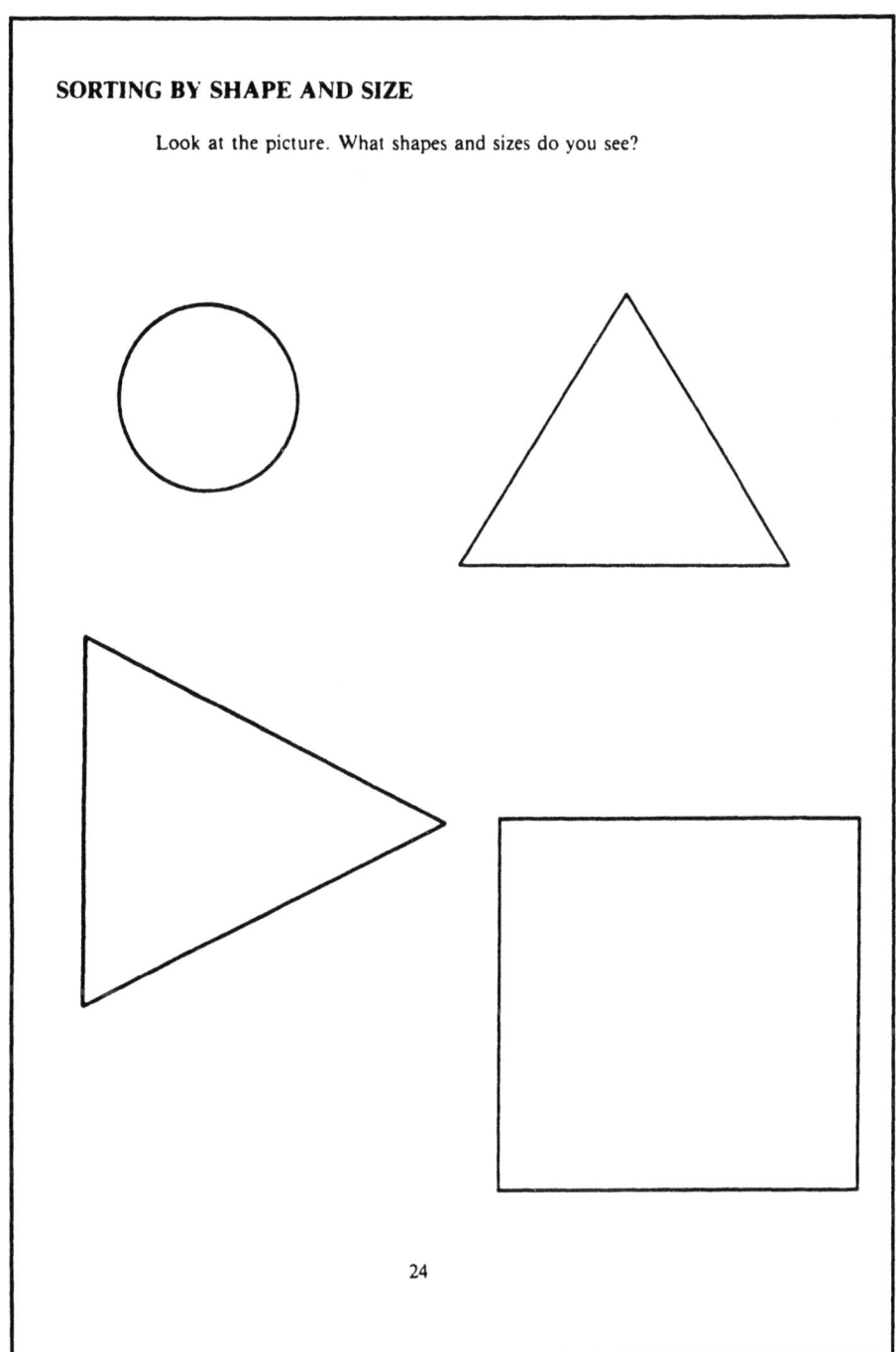

ACTIVITY FIVE: Sorting by Shape and Size

Ask your students to turn to page 24. Read aloud the text on this page. Engage your students in naming what they see on this page and the following one. Be sure that students have named the shapes - triangle, square, and circle - and named the sizes - large, medium, and small.

Hand out the copies of pages 24-25, and have your students cut out the shapes from the copies.

Now ask your students to play with the shapes on their desks, arranging them into different groups or categories. Tell them they can arrange them however they like and they may keep changing the groups. Walk around, and look at the groupings.

Next have students turn to page 26. Tell them that both Carlos and Sara have the same kind of shapes that they have. In the pictures Carlos and Sara are both sorting their shapes onto different shelves.

Read aloud the directions on the top half of the page. Explain that Carlos has put all of his large shapes on the top shelf, the medium ones on the middle shelf, and the small ones on the bottom shelf. Ask your students to sort their shapes like Carlos did. After they have done this, say that the students have just put their shapes into groups or categories based on size: small, medium, and large.

Now ask students to look at bottom of the page. Read the text aloud. Say that Sara has put all her square shapes on the top shelf, all her triangle shapes on the middle shelf, and all her circle shapes on the bottom shelf. Ask your students to sort their shapes like Sara did. After they have done this, say that they have just put their shapes into groups or categories based on shape: square, triangle, and circle.

Explain to your students that often we can fit the same things into many different categories.

Now give your students crayons, plain paper, and glue. Ask them to color or decorate their shapes first and then to make a collage, arranging the shapes any way they like on the paper. Have them begin.

When your students have finished with their collages, ask them to share what they have done with a partner or a small group.

Approximate Time: 25 TO 30 MINUTES

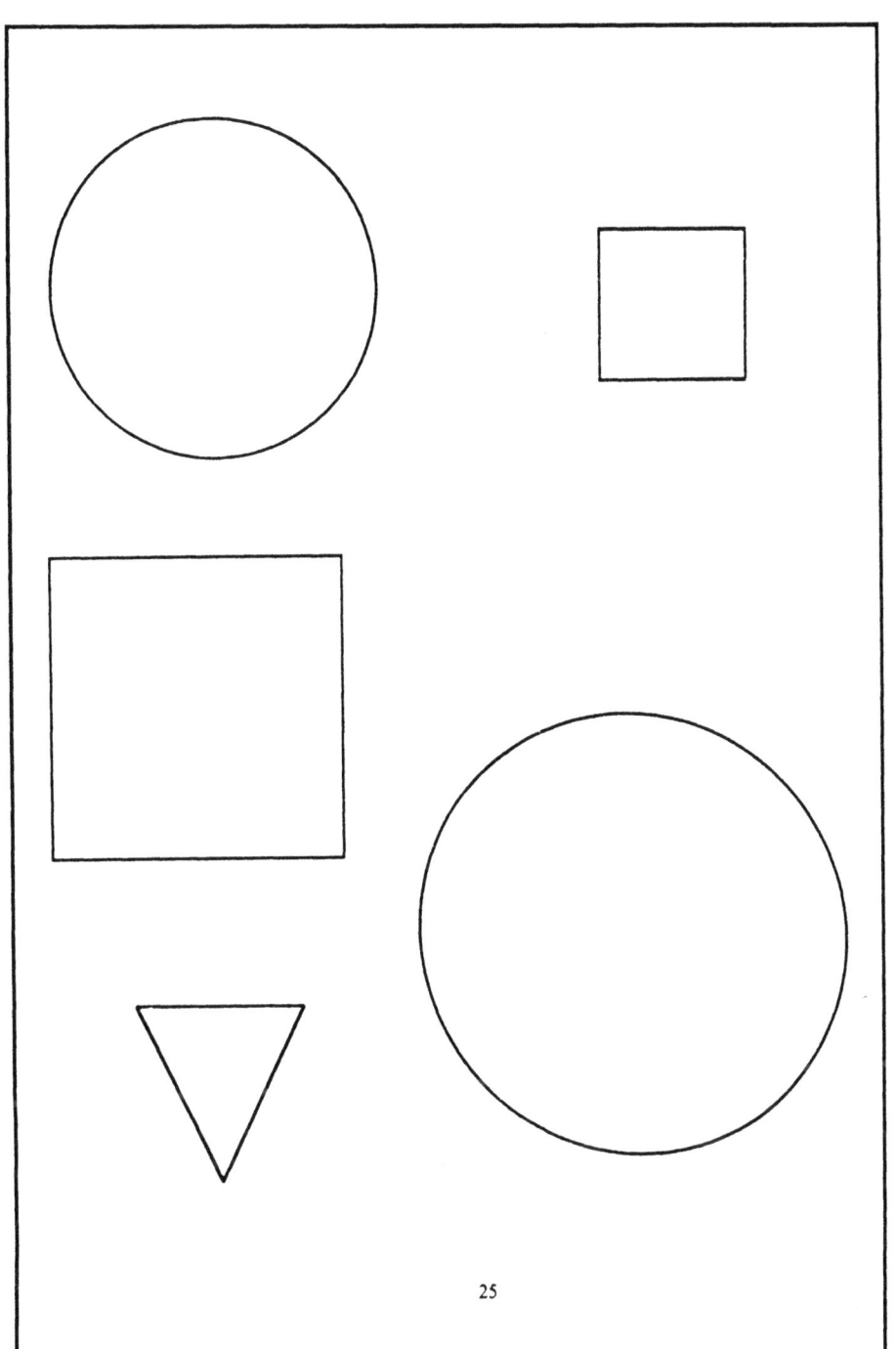

SORTING BY SIZE AND SHAPE

Carlos is sorting his shapes. Sort your shapes like Carlos.

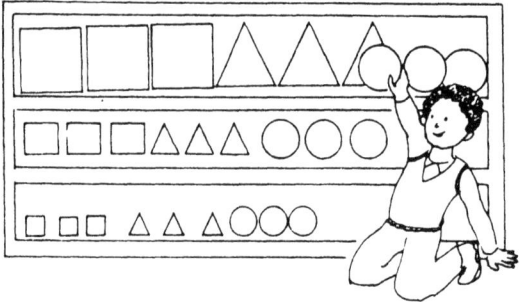

Sara is sorting her shapes. Sort your shapes like Sara.

26

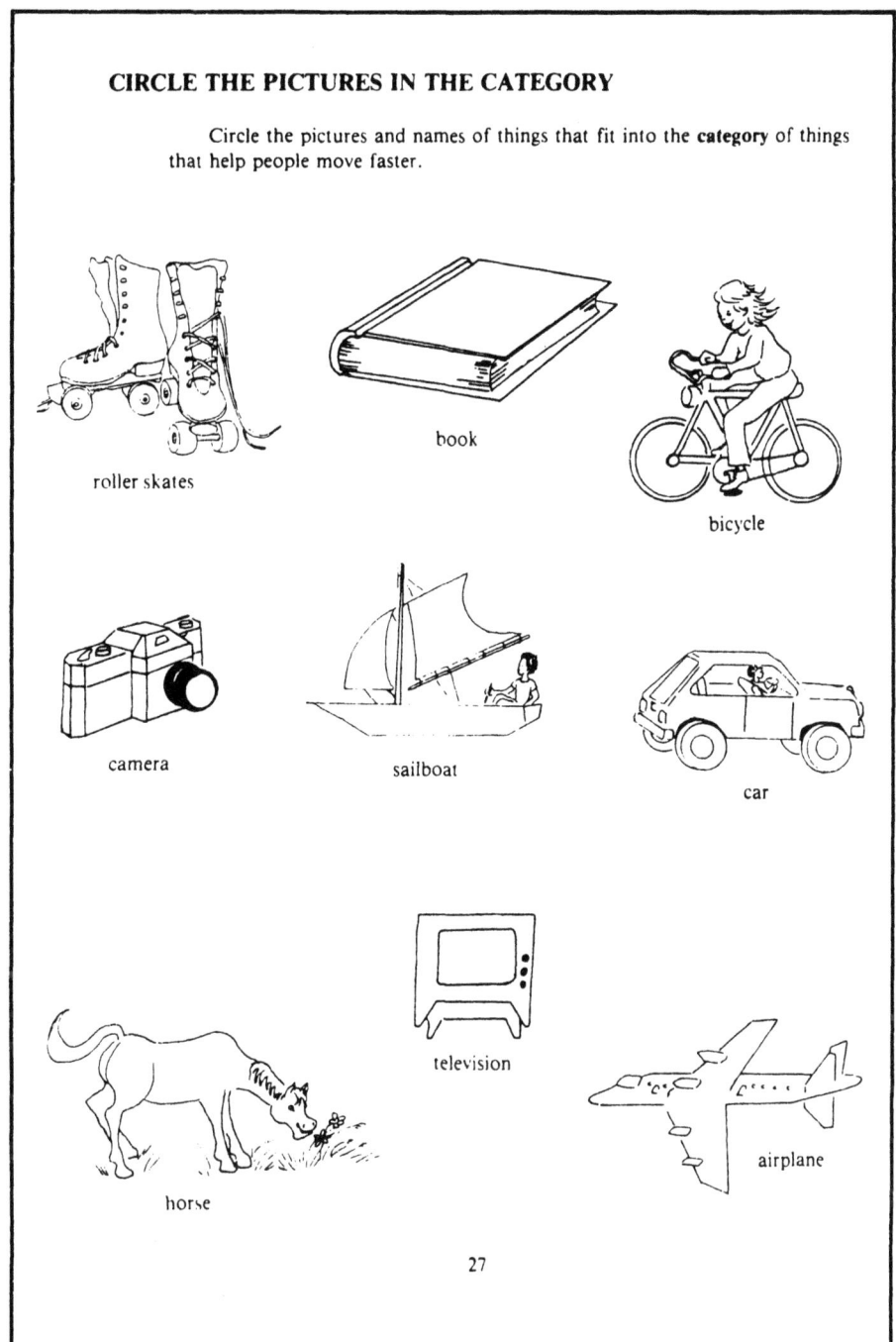

ACTIVITY SIX: Circle the Pictures in the Category

Ask your students to turn to page 27. Ask them to name the pictures on the page. Tell them that the pictures on this page can fit into many different categories. Ask them to circle only the pictures of things that fit into the category of things that are used to help a person travel faster.

Allow the students time to follow instructions. Ask your students, **"Who circled roller skates?"** Ask them how roller skates can help a person travel faster. Do the same for each object. Be sure all students understand why all items except for camera, television, and book should be circled.

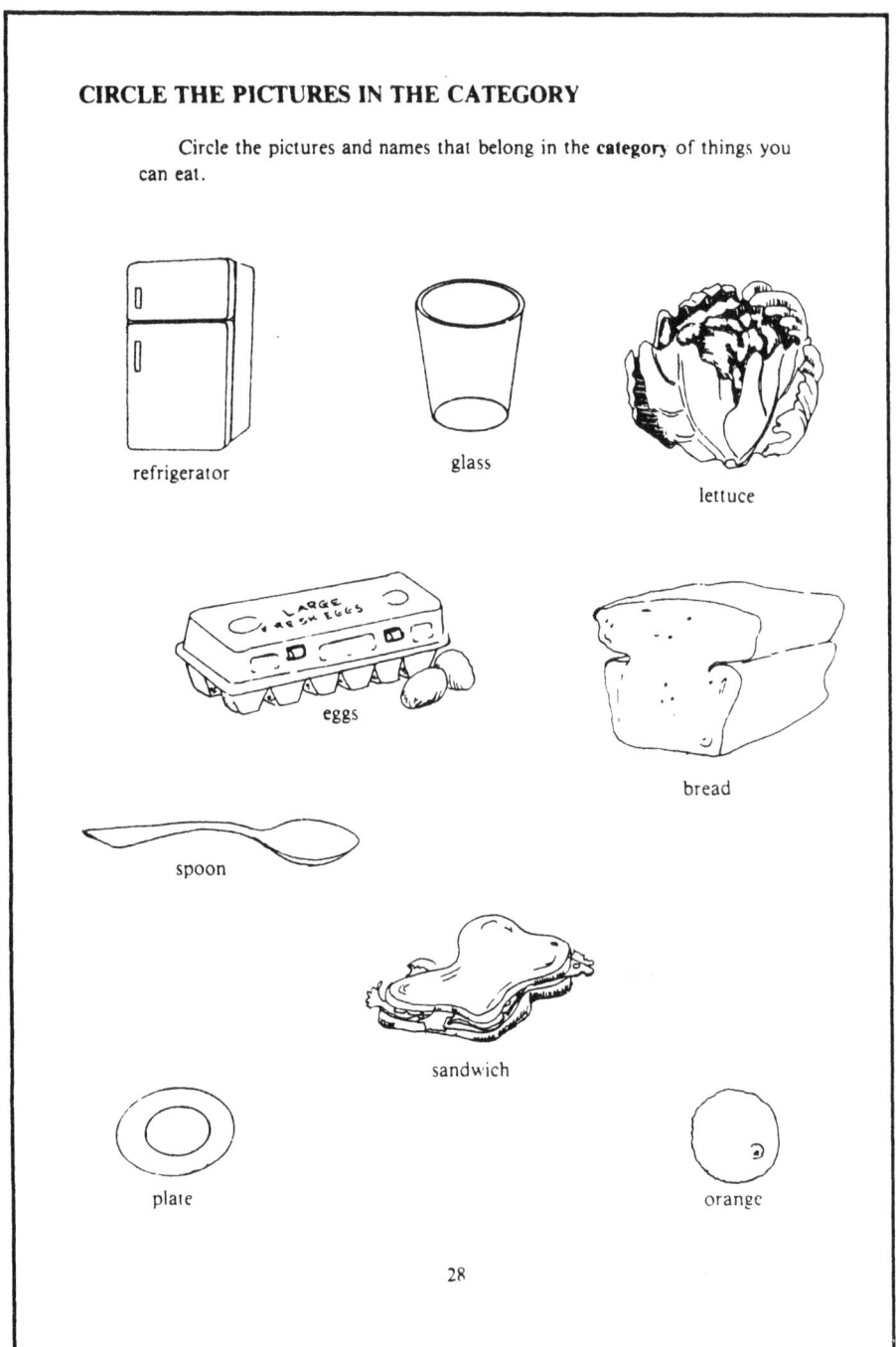

Now ask your students to turn to page 28. Ask them to name the pictures that belong in the category of things you can eat. Give the students time to do this.

Ask your students to name the objects that they circled. Talk about how spoon, glass, plate, and refrigerator are related to the category of food but are not objects in the category of food and should not be circled.

Approximate Time: 5 TO 10 MINUTES

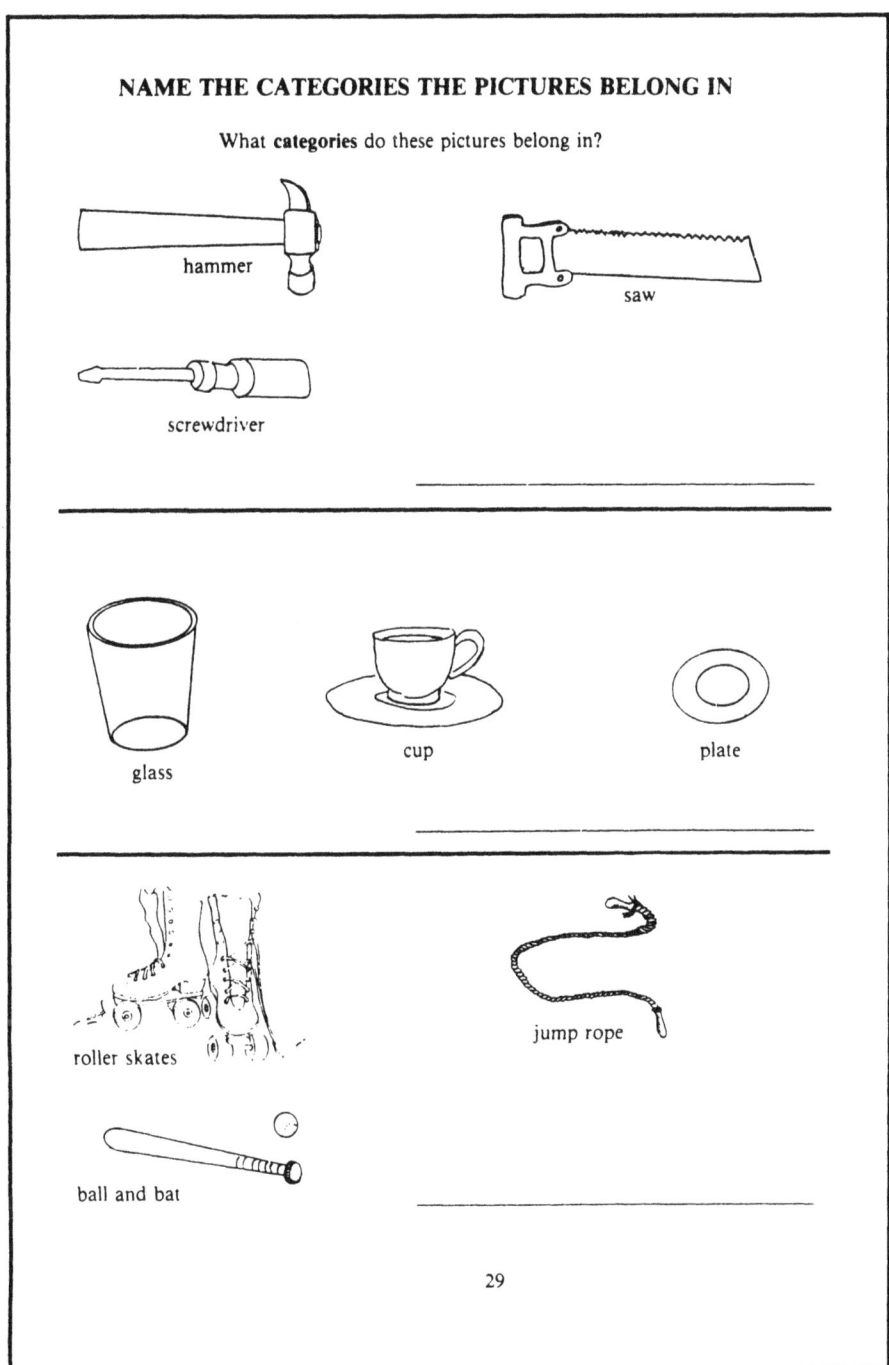

ACTIVITY SEVEN: Name the Categories the Pictures Belong In

Tell your students to turn to page 29. Ask them to name the pictures in the top section of the page. Ask what category these pictures belong in. Wait until someone says *tools*. If a student responds with *things to build with,* say, **"That's right, but what is another name for things to build with?"** If your students' writing skills allow, ask them to write the category name on the line to the right of the pictures. You can write it on the blackboard first. Follow the same procedure for the bottom sections.

Approximate Time: 5 TO 10 MINUTES

ACTIVITY EIGHT: Categorizing Students

You will need a space where all of the students in your classroom can stand or sit in groups, apart from the desks. Gather your students in this space, and tell them that you are going to put them into two different categories.

Call all of the boys' names. Have them stand in one area. Then call all of the girls' names, and have them stand in another area. Ask the students what categories you have used to divide them. Elicit the categories *boys* and *girls.*

Now say that you want all of the students who fit into the category of children who have brothers or sisters to stand in a certain place. Then say that you want all of the students who have no brothers or sisters to stand in another place. Ask your students to repeat what categories they are standing in.

Using these two methods – 1) organizing children by category and asking them to identify the category, and 2) naming a category and asking students to put themselves in the right one – categorize your students in a number of different ways. You can make up your own categories, ask students to make up some, and/or use some of the following:

  a. hair color
  b. eye color
  c. shoe color
  d. shirt color
  e. favorite ice cream flavor
  f. favorite outdoor activity
  g. favorite animal

Approximate Time: 10 TO 15 MINUTES

ACTIVITY NINE: Dramatizing Categories

Divide the class into groups of four students. Announce that you will be dramatizing things in different categories. Say that the first category will be FOODS. Give each group a piece of paper on which is written an item in that category. If the students can't read it, you can tell them secretly. Tell each group they can work together to think of ways to act out eating their food. Then let each group perform in front of the whole class while the class guesses which food is being acted out.

CATEGORY: Foods

THINGS TO DRAMATIZE:
- Eating spaghetti
- Peeling and eating a banana
- Eating watermelon and spitting out seeds
- Making and eating a peanut butter sandwich
- Peeling and eating an orange
- Eating an ice cream cone
- Putting catsup on French fries and eating them
- Eating rice with chopsticks

Repeat the above directions for the Occupations category.

CATEGORY: Occupations

THINGS TO DRAMATIZE:
- Airplane Pilot
- Fire Fighter
- Doctor
- Teacher
- Cook
- Truck Driver
- Construction Worker
- Farmer
- Waitperson

You may want to think of other categories to dramatize.

Approximate Time: 20 TO 25 MINUTES

ADDITIONAL ACTIVITIES FOR UNIT 4

CATEGORIZING A VARIETY OF REAL OBJECTS: COMMERCIALLY PREPARED

For young children to understand the concept of categorizing, it is very important that they have the experience of categorizing real objects. You may have in your classroom a variety of commercially made items for this purpose. Suggested items include the following: blocks, cuisenaire rods, concept attainment blocks, math counting sets, play money sets, and so on. Your students need ongoing opportunities to work with these items throughout the school year.

CATEGORIZING A VARIETY OF REAL OBJECTS: FOUND OBJECTS

Collect a variety of objects to keep in an accessible place in your classroom. Store them in tubs or buckets. Some suggestions for this are bottle caps, sea shells, stones, buttons, various types of macaroni, and so on. Encourage your students to experiment freely with finding different categories in which to sort these objects. Talk about the categories formed.

CATEGORY WALK 1

Take your students on a walk. Give every student a paper bag to bring along. Say that you will be collecting things that you will put into categories when you return to the classroom. Look for stones, sticks, weeds, papers, and so on. When you return, allow each student to categorize her/his things individually. Then have each student share one of her/his catgeories and its objects. After this activity you may have the students group their objects together to form larger collections in each category.

CATEGORY WALK 2

Before you go on a walk, have your students think of categories of things that they might see on a walk around the school. Categories might include kinds of colors of cars, kinds of trees, kinds of people (male, female, young, old), kinds of stores, kinds of things to play with, and so on. Divide the students into groups of four or more, and assign each group a category. Have each group report to the whole class when you return. List the items in each category on the board.

CATEGORY GAME

There are many slightly different versions of the category game. Before using this one, ask your students if anyone knows the game, giving a simple description of it. If your students know the game, you may want to use the version that most of them know.

The game is played in a rhythm, and the rhythm must not be broken. The entire group first slaps thighs twice, then claps hands twice, then snaps fingers twice, once on each hand, saying "CATE" on the right snap and "GORY" on the left snap. The person who has been designated to start then names a category, such as animals, toys, girls, foods, books, and so on. The entire rhythm is repeated, and the first person then names an object in that category. The entire rhythm is repeated again, and the next person names a different object in that category, and so on. The SLAP SLAP CLAP CLAP SNAP SNAP rhythm is never broken. Anytime someone cannot think of another object in that category and wants to change categories, that person says "CATEGORY" in her/his turn and then names an object in that category. The next person names a different object in that category, and so on.

CATEGORY MURAL OR COLLAGE

Decide on a particular category such as PETS, FARM ANIMALS, TRANSPORTATION, OCCUPATIONS, or SPORTS. Provide a very large piece of paper. Give students magazines, and ask them to find and cut out pictures that fit into the chosen category. Ask students to paste or tape pictures on the large piece of paper. An alternative is to ask students to draw pictures that fit into the selected category, making a mural that illustrates it. Or ask students to make individual murals or collages.

CATEGORIZING LIBRARY BOOKS

Have partners or small groups of children categorize library books according to one category at a time, such as size, color, or subject matter. Ask other children to guess the category.

UNIT **5**

Put It In Order

Introduction

Sequencing or putting things in an order is often required if students are to understand the meaning of a group of things. Sequencing involves all the previous skills: listening, observing, understanding what needs to be done, and categorizing. In this unit the word *order* will be used to mean sequence.

Students intuitively understand that there is an order to their day, their life, and the world. They understand that they get up before they eat breakfast and that they get dressed before they go to school. They also understand that some of their friends are older or younger and taller or shorter than they are. Patterning is a precursor skill to sequencing. Activities that teach patterning have been included as initial exercises in this unit. The purpose of this unit is to increase your students' awareness of order and sequence in their daily lives and its importance in their academic lives.

Approximate Time for Unit 5: 90 TO 140 MINUTES

You will want to teach this unit and all of the units in more than one session, with periods of no more than 30 to 35 minutes.

There are many possible ways of scheduling this unit. You might teach it in daily periods during one week. You could teach Activities #1, #2, and #3 on one day; #4 and #5 on the next; #6 and #7 on the following day; and #8 and #9, and #10 on the next. On the fifth day you might choose from ADDITIONAL ACTIVITIES at the end of the unit. You may want to include ADDITIONAL ACTIVITIES at other times during the day or use them to extend the unit into the following week.

If you choose to teach this unit in shorter periods, you could teach fewer activities on each day and extend the time spent on this unit to two weeks.

> UNIT **5**
>
> # Put It In Order
>
> **Introduction**
>
> You can put things in order by:
>
> age
> size
> color
>
> To put in order means that one thing comes before another. It is a way to organize things.
>
>
>
> 30

SUGGESTED ACTIVITIES FOR UNIT 5

ACTIVITY ONE: What Do We Mean by "Put It In Order"?

Begin by telling your students that they will be talking about order.

Ask your students to turn to page 30 in their **Programs.** Read aloud and discuss the *Introduction*. Make sure that your students understand that *order* means one thing coming after another. Say that you will be doing some activities to help them learn how to put things in order.

Approximate Time: 3 TO 5 MINUTES

ACTIVITY TWO: Look at Our Pencils!

Ask your students to put their pencils on their desks. Tell them that they are going to line up their pencils from the shortest to the longest. Ask them to look at the various lengths of the pencils. Give them 20 seconds to look around at the pencils on the desks. Begin by asking two or three students to bring their pencils to the front of the class. Arrange the pencils on a table or on the floor in order from the shortest to the longest. Then ask two more students to place their pencils where they belong in the order. Continue this activity until all pencils are in order from the shortest to the longest.

Approximate Time: 5 TO 10 MINUTES

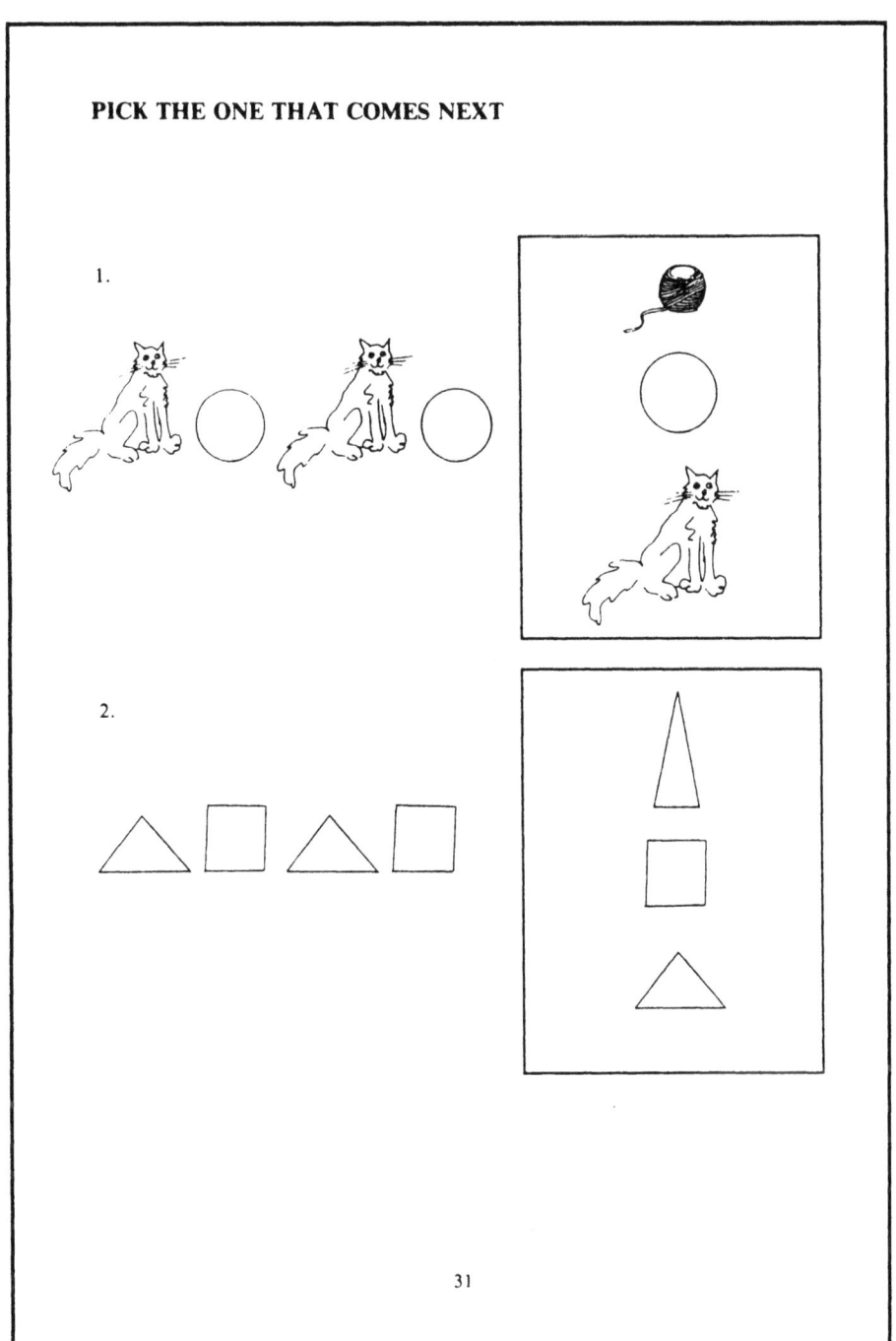

ACTIVITY THREE: Pick the One that Comes Next

Tell your students to turn to page 31. Ask them to look at the order of the pictures in #1. Ask one student to say aloud the order. Instruct them to circle the shape in the box that comes next. Have a volunteer give the correct answer.

Follow the same procedure for #2 - #5.

Approximate Time: 5 TO 10 MINUTES

3.

4.

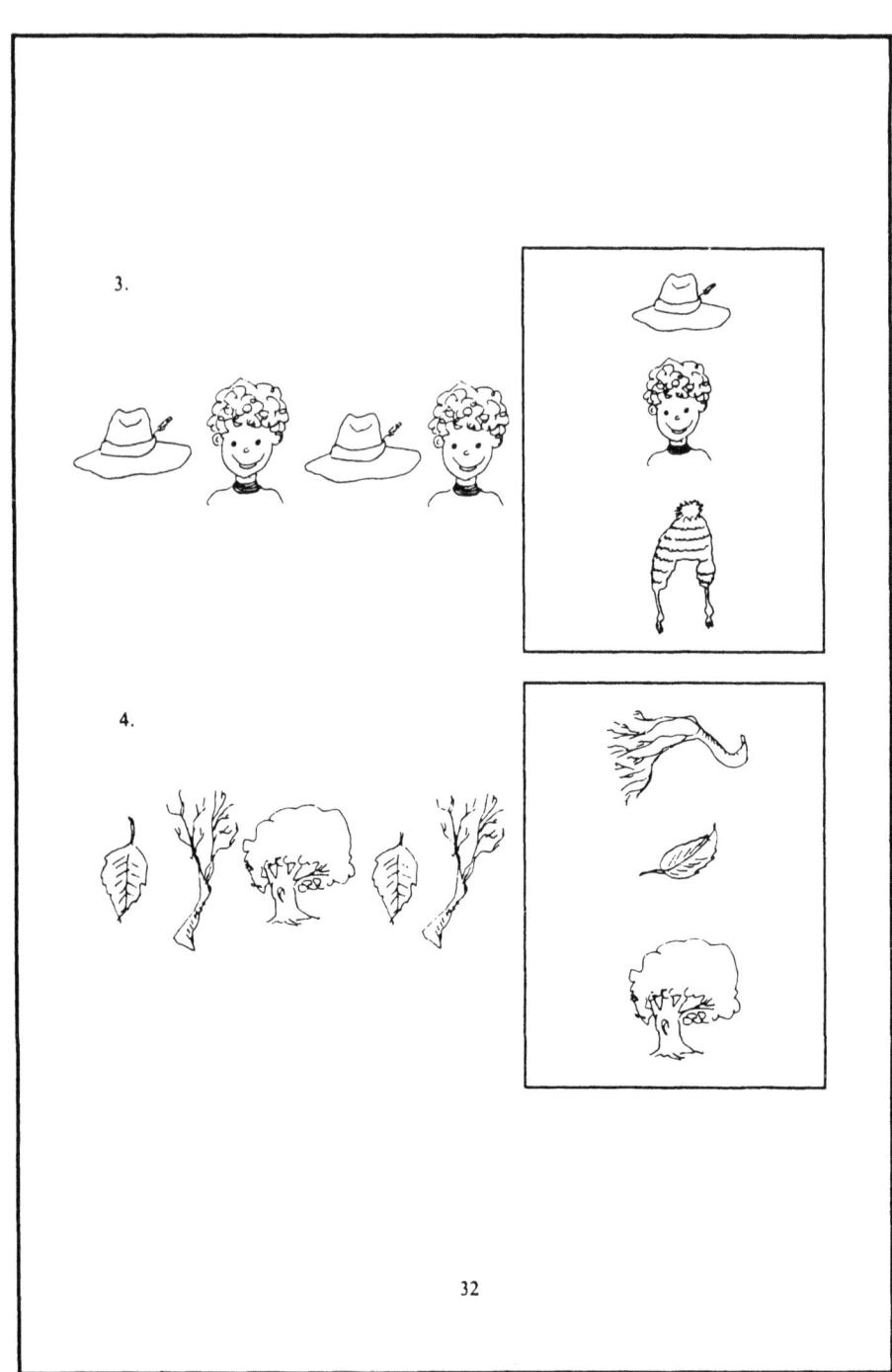

5.

ACTIVITY FOUR: Put It in Order

Instruct your students to turn to page 34. Ask them to look at the pictures in the first box. Tell them that these pictures can be rearranged so that they will be in order. Ask them to put the pictures in order by drawing them in the space provided. Accept the order they provide, either small to large or large to small.

Follow the same procedure for #2 - #5.

Approximate Time: 5 TO 10 MINUTES

3.

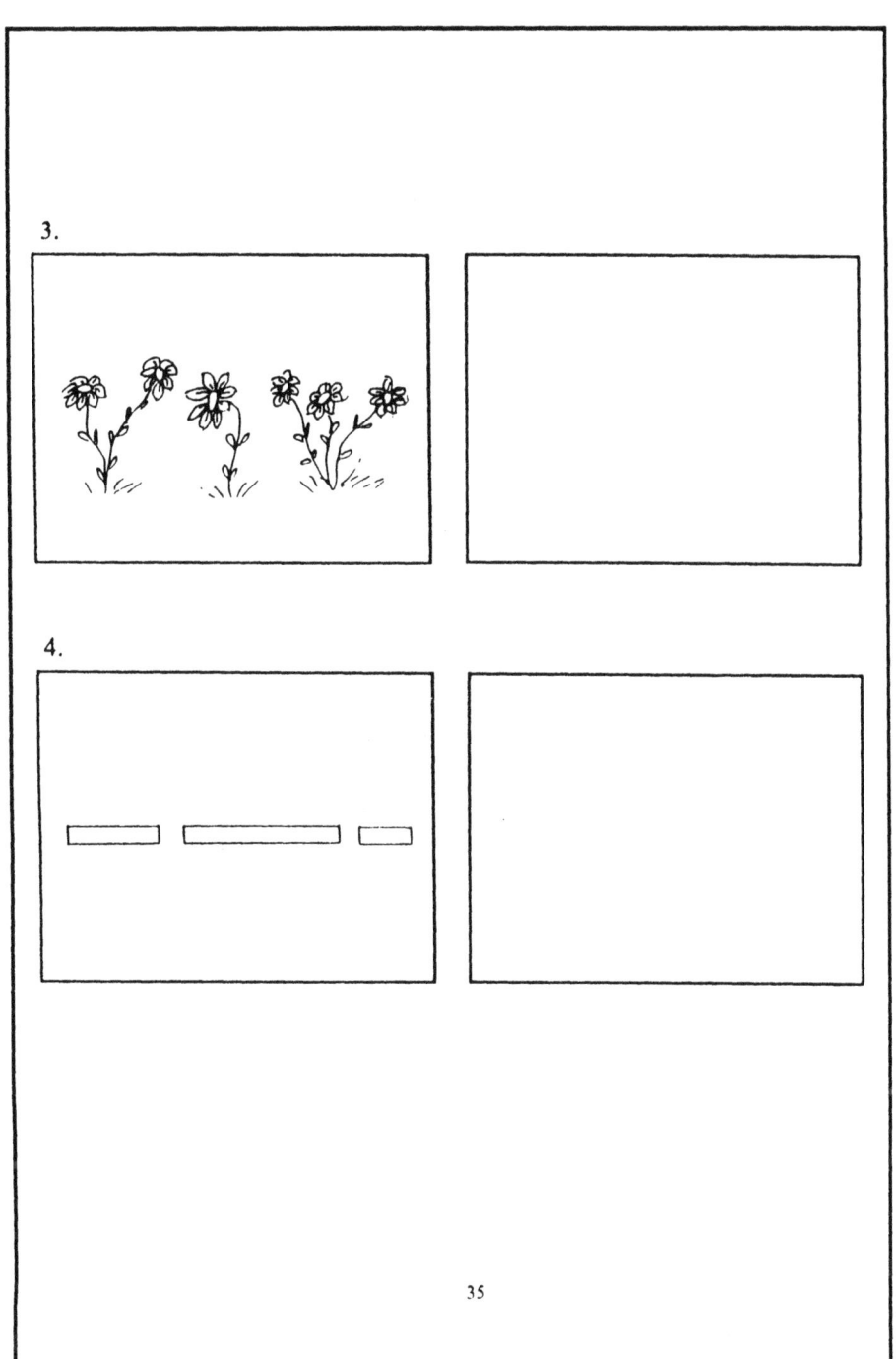

4.

ACTIVITY FIVE: Sequence a Story

Have drawing paper and crayons available to students. Tell your students that you are going to tell them a story. Tell them that you would like them to listen carefully to the story. Explain that when it is over, you will ask them the order of what happened. Read the story slowly.

Picking Blueberries

One morning I awoke very early. Buzzy, my dog, was still asleep next to my bed. I was very hungry so I went to the cupboard and took out a box of cereal. I put the cereal in a bowl and poured milk over it. I ate it all up. I wanted some blueberries. I grabbed a bucket and went for a walk down the trail. Buzzy sleepily followed along. I found the blueberry patch and began to pick the berries until the bucket overflowed. I ate a few too. I took the blueberries home. I washed them and put them in a cereal bowl to eat. Then I ate them.

Ask the students what happened first in the story. Choose students to illustrate this event, and have them begin to draw. Ask other students to list the remaining events of the story. Choose students to illustrate these events, and have them do so. When all the students have completed their drawings, arrange them in the order of the story.

Now ask your students if they could order the events of the story in a different way. Allow them time to give you different sequences of events. Rearrange their illustrations as they tell the story in a different way. Discuss with them how ordering in different ways changes the meaning of the story.

Approximate Time: 15 TO 20 MINUTES

ACTIVITY SIX: Group Story

Ask students to tell you the order in which they must leave the room for a fire drill. Ask them what they must do first. Have them tell you the sequence of all the actions they must take. Remind them that these actions must occur in order for all of the children to leave the room safely.

Now tell the students that you are going to write a group story together. Ask them for suggestions, about starting the story. Choose one of their suggestions, or begin with your own such as "Jane and Rico were playing ball..." Ask your students what happened next. Write their answers on the board or a large sheet of paper. Continue the story by asking, "What happened next?" Follow this procedure until the story is finished.

Allow your students time to draw a picture to illustrate the story or parts of the story. Display their pictures with the story they have written so they can read it themselves when they have time.

Approximate Time: 15 TO 20 MINUTES

ACTIVITY SEVEN: Dramatize an Event

Arrange your students in pairs. Tell them that they are going to act out an event for the rest of the class without using words. Show them an example: pantomime that you are making a snowball and rolling it into a big snowman. Ask them to tell you the different steps that you are pantomiming.

Assign each group an event to pantomime. Some suggestions include the following: picking a bouquet of flowers; getting a glass of water and drinking it; setting the table for dinner; reading a book from beginning to end; climbing a tree; making a bed; mixing batter and making cookies; shoveling snow; flying a kite.

Give your students two minutes to practice their sequence. Have the pairs take turns presenting their event to the whole class. Have the class guess the kind of event and the order of its actions.

Approximate Time: 15 TO 20 MINUTES

ACTIVITY EIGHT: Order the Pictures

Ask your students to turn to page 37. Instruct them to look at the pictures in #1 and arrange the pictures in order by numbering them from 1 to 3. Discuss their answers, and accept any reasonable sequence.

Follow the same procedure for #2 - #9.

Approximate Time: 10 TO 15 MINUTES

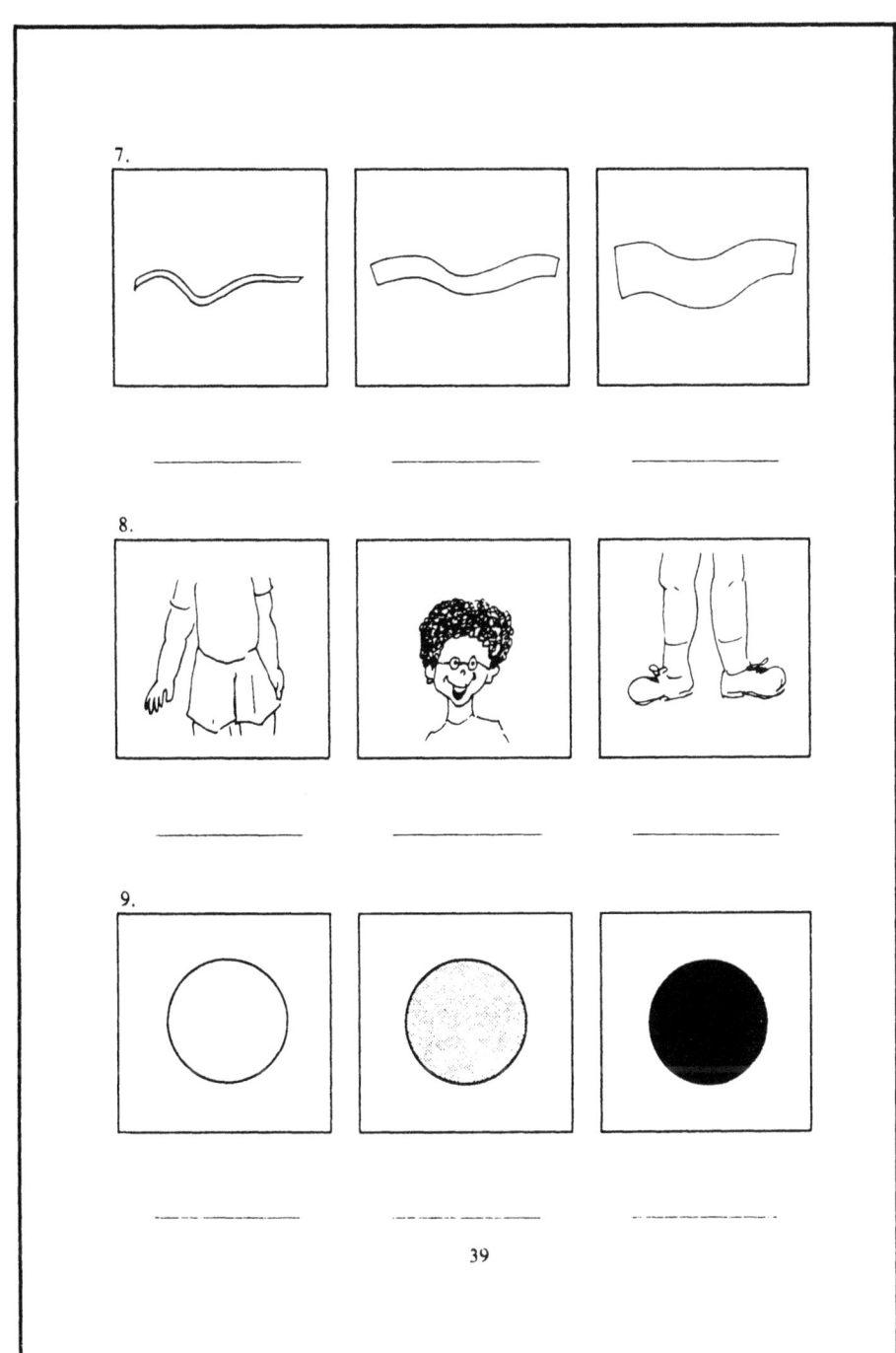

FINISH THE PICTURE

40

ACTIVITY NINE: Finish the Picture

Ask your students to turn to page 40 in their **Programs.** Ask them to look at the picture at the top of the page. Discuss with them what is happening in the picture. Ask them to draw a picture of what will happen next using the white space on page 40. Allow your students time to share their stories with the whole class.

Approximate Time: 10 TO 15 MINUTES

CREATE THE ACTION

1. It is Halloween Night. First I...

2. Then I...

3. Finally I...

41

ACTIVITY TEN: Create the Action

Ask students to turn to page 41. Tell them that they are going to create their own stories by drawing the action in the three spaces provided. Read to them the statement above space #1. Ask them to draw a picture in that space. Allow them about two minutes to do so. Read to them the statement above space #2. Tell them that space #2 should contain a picture of what happened next. Allow them time to draw this picture. Follow the same procedure for space #3.

Allow students time to share their stories with the class. Discuss the stories and the order of the events.

Approximate Time: 10 TO 15 MINUTES

ADDITIONAL ACTIVITIES FOR UNIT 5

NATURE WALK

Take your class for a walk around the school yard. Collect things along the way. When you return to your classroom, have your students order the things you've collected by size from smallest to largest, by shade from dullest to brightest, by texture from smoothest to roughest, etc. You can also make a chart that retraces your steps in the sequence you traveled.

FIELD TRIP

Take your students on a field trip to a place where something is being made, such as an ice cream factory, a pottery shop, or an automobile plant. When you return to the classroom, have your students write a story about where they went and the order of the events they observed. They can also make a picture book about the steps needed to make the thing that they observed.

CALENDAR TIME

Each morning discuss the day of the week and the month of the year with your students. Include in this discussion the names of the days and months that came before and after this one. Have a schedule of the day written on the board, and review it with your students each morning.

COOKING

Plan cooking activities with your students. Discuss the ingredients and the order necessary for preparation of the food.

NUMBER SEQUENCE

During each day have students count using ordinal as well as cardinal numbers. Have them tell you who is the first, second, third, etc. in line; which book is the first, second, third on the shelf; which letter is first, second, third in the alphabet, etc.

SAY THE WORD THAT CONTINUES THE SEQUENCE

Tell your students that you are going to play a game. You will give them two words that suggest an order. They are to provide the third word that follows the first two. Read the following words to them:

- Monday, Tuesday, _____.
- Tall, medium, _____.
- One, two, _____.
- 1st grade, 2nd grade, _____.
- Small, medium, _____.
- Day, month, _____.

UNIT 6

Pictures In Your Mind

Introduction

The ability to see "pictures in your mind" or to *visualize* is the ability to use the imagination to form mental images. One of the definitions of imagination given in *Webster's Dictionary* is the following: 1) "the act or power of forming a mental image of something not present to the senses or never before wholly perceived in reality." By allowing us to hold a mental image of something not physically present, imagination is the tool that enables us to think abstractly as well as concretely. Without the ability to imagine, children could not read, do math problems, or master geography. Visualization helps students to comprehend and retain information.

When teachers understand the central role of visualization in their students' learning, they engage their students in activities that support and develop these skills. They know that these imaging skills will help students to learn and achieve in all subjects.

A second *Webster's Dictionary* definition of imagination is simply "creative ability." The ability to imagine is the basis of all creative discovery, both artistic and scientific. Adult geniuses in all fields have both mastered the content of their disciplines and have retained active imaginations. The imagination allows a person to see ideas and information in original ways. Adults who have made significant contributions to their fields often report new discoveries stemming from a visual image that reframes a problem in a completely new framework. All of your students can learn to be creative thinkers in the various areas of their lives. Practice in visualization skills will help your students to become more creative thinkers.

The activities in this unit are designed to encourage and improve visualization skills. Note that the purpose of Activity #6 is to improve students' ability to retain information.

In each of the activities in this unit, students are asked to close their eyes. This allows children to visualize without visual distraction from the environment. However, some students will find it difficult to keep their eyes closed for the entire activity. You may want to remind students to close their eyes, but it is not essential that they do so. Some students are able to visualize without closing their eyes. The main concern is that the students are quiet and calm.

Approximate Time for Unit 6: 85 TO 115 MINUTES

You'll want to teach this unit and all of the units in more than one session, with periods of no more than 30 to 35 minutes. You could teach Activities #1 and #2 on one day; #3 on the next; #4 on the following day; #5 on the next, and #6 on the fifth. You may want to include ADDITIONAL ACTIVITIES at other times during the day or use them to extend the unit into the following week.

UNIT **6**

Pictures In Your Mind

Introduction

Your mind is thinking all the time.

Sometimes you think in words, and sometimes you think in pictures.

Sometimes the pictures in your mind are clear, and sometimes they are cloudy or fuzzy.

When the pictures in your mind are clear and easy to see, your mind can think better.

The activities in this unit will help you to see clearer pictures in your mind.

What do you see in this picture?

42

SUGGESTED ACTIVITIES FOR UNIT 6

ACTIVITY ONE: Seeing Pictures in Your Mind

Ask your students to turn to page 42. Read aloud the *Introduction,* and discuss the picture. Tell the students that Juan, Stephanie, James, and Yolanda are closing their eyes and seeing pictures in their minds of their favorite toys. Ask your students to name the kinds of toys that the children in the picture are seeing.

Now give these directions to your students: **"Close your eyes like the students in the picture. Try to see a picture in your mind of your favorite toy. Keep your eyes closed, and look at your toy quietly for a moment, until I tell you to open your eyes...** (Pause for approximately fifteen seconds.) **Now open your eyes."** Ask if students saw their toys. Allow students who did to tell what kind of toys they saw.

Approximate Time: 5 TO 10 MINUTES

ACTIVITY TWO: A Trip to the Beach

Ask students how many of them have been to the beach or seen pictures of the beach. Ask them to raise their hands in response to this question. Lead a short discussion about beaches, allowing students to give information about their knowledge of beaches.

Then read aloud the following, pausing for a few seconds between each sentence.

"We are going to take a pretend trip to the beach. Close your eyes and try to see pictures in your mind. Imagine that it is a very warm, sunny day, and you are sitting on a sandy beach.. You are wearing a swimming suit... Feel the hot sun on your legs... Feel the warm, soft sand with your hands... See the blue water with the waves hitting the beach... Hear the sound of the waves... Look around you and see if there are animals or birds or other people on the beach with you... If there are, watch what they are doing... Now imagine that you get up and walk slowly down to the water... Put your feet in the water and feel if it is warm or cool... Now slowly turn around and walk out of the water. Now we are going to leave the beach and come back to the classroom. Slowly open your eyes..."

Ask your students if they saw pictures of the beach in their minds. Ask questions about what they imagined. Give each student who wants to talk time to share one thing.

Approximate Time: 15 TO 20 MINUTES

THE STRANGE ANIMAL

What do you see in this picture?

43

ACTIVITY THREE: The Strange Animal

Ask your students to turn to page 43. Also hand out a variety of colors of crayons to each student. Ask students to tell about what is in the picture. When they have identified that it is a boy pointing to something and they have named the animals in the picture, ask them to close their eyes while you tell them a short story. Ask them to see pictures of the story in their minds while you read. Read the following:

"One day Jeremy went walking through the woods in back of his house. He wanted to see the birds, insects, and animals that live in the woods. He walked slowly and quietly and looked all around. First he heard a rustling sound in a tree and looked up to see a grey squirrel looking down at him. "Hi, squirrel," he said, and the squirrel chattered back. He walked on until he saw some yellow flowers and heard a buzzing sound in them. He looked closely and saw a yellow and black striped bee circling the flowers. "Hi, bee," he whispered. The bee buzzed back. He heard a chirping sound above his head, and he noticed a black bird sitting on a branch. "Hi, bird," he sang, and the bird seemed to chirp "Hello" back. Then suddenly the strangest animal Jeremy had ever seen came walking up to him. Jeremy stared and stared. He couldn't believe his eyes.

"That's the end of the story, but I want you to keep your eyes closed and see the strange animal that comes walking up to Jeremy. Notice exactly how it looks. See what color it is, how big it is, how its head looks, how its body looks, how its feet or paws look, if it has a tail, and anything else that you can notice. Keep seeing the picture of the animal in your mind... (Pause for about fifteen seconds.) **Now slowly open your eyes and begin to draw the strange animal that you saw. Draw it on page 43 — in the place that Jeremy is pointing.**"

Allow time for the students to complete their drawings. When your students are done, ask them to show and share information about their drawings with the students seated near them. Comment about the interesting variety of strange animals that they saw as pictures in their minds.

Approximate Time: 15 TO 20 MINUTES

ACTIVITY FOUR: What Is in the Treasure Chest?

Ask your students to turn to page 44. Have them look at the picture. Read the question under the picture. Allow students time to describe what they see in the picture. Make sure that they understand that the children in the picture are finding a hidden treasure chest.

Then read the remaining directions on the page. Ask your students to follow the directions. Tell them to remain completely quiet with their eyes closed while they see pictures in their minds of things that they think might be in the treasure chest. Tell them that they can see whatever they want. Tell them that they can see many things or just a few things. Ask students to notice exactly what the things in their treasure chest look like. Ask them to notice how big each thing is and what color it is. Allow approximately one or two minutes for this process.

Now ask your students to open their eyes but to keep what they saw in their treasure chests a secret for a few more minutes. Ask them to turn to page 45. Supply each student with crayons in a variety of colors. Tell students to draw pictures of the things that they imagined were in their treasure chests. Allow about five minutes for students to complete their drawings, extending this time if many students are still drawing.

Now have students work with partners or in small groups to share their pictures of treasure. Allow a few minutes for each child to show and tell about what she/he imagined was in her/his treasure chest.

Finally ask the entire class to share. Let each student name one thing that was in her/his treasure chest while you make a list on the blackboard or on a large sheet of paper. Point out that students saw many different kinds of pictures in their minds.

Approximate Time: 20 TO 25 MINUTES

WHAT IS IN THE TREASURE CHEST?

Draw what you saw in the picture in your mind.

ACTIVITY FIVE: Seeing Pictures of Real Things

Ask your students to close their eyes. Read aloud the following directions:

"Close your eyes. Try to see a picture in your mind of the outside of our school building. Notice what color is it, what it is built of, what the door looks like, what the windows look like. (Modify to fit description of your school.) **Take a moment to try to see how our school looks."**

Ask your students to open their eyes. Have them describe the school.

Then read aloud these directions.

"Now close your eyes again. This time try to see a picture in your mind of the front of the outside of the house or apartment building you live in. Try to see exactly how it looks. See its shape. Notice what color it is and what the windows and doors look like. Take a moment to see as many things as you can about how your house looks."

Ask your students to open their eyes. Lead a discussion of their experiences. Ask if they could see a picture of their house or building in their mind. Allow each student to tell one thing about his or her house or building.

Then read aloud these directions.

"Now I want you to try to see a picture in your mind of the room that you sleep in at home. Notice what your bed looks like. Notice what color the walls of the room are. Are there pictures or anything else on the walls? Look at the floor of the room. What color is it? Is there a rug? Do you see any of your toys in this room? What else do you see? Keep your eyes closed and look at the room." (Pause for about fifteen seconds.) **"Now open your eyes."**

Ask your students if they could see a picture in their minds of the room where they sleep. Let each student tell one thing about her/his room.

Approximate Time: 15 TO 20 MINUTES

ACTIVITY SIX: The Queen Who Learned to Listen

Tell your students that you are going to read them a story. Tell them that you want them to close their eyes while you read the story. Ask them to try to see pictures of the story in their minds while you read. Now read the following story slowly.

The Queen Who Learned to Listen

Once long ago there lived a Queen named Queen Big. She was called that because she was very tall. She lived in a bright purple castle with her white dog named Snowball who slept in a little bed next to her big bed.

In most ways Queen Big was a good queen. She was kind to the people in her kingdom and made sure that they always had plenty of food to eat, especially pizza, their favorite food. She gave each family a purple house to live in that was the same color as her castle.

Queen Big had only one problem. She didn't know how to listen to other people. She liked to talk so much that she talked all the time. After a while people got tired of hearing her talk. They wished she would listen to them for a change. They tried to stay away from her, even though she was a nice queen. They hid behind trees when they saw her. Queen Big began to get very lonely. Only her dog Snowball listened to her, but sometimes at night he fell asleep in his little bed while she was talking.

One morning Queen Big woke up and found that she couldn't talk. This scared her. She sent for Doctor Small, who came and examined her. Doctor Small told her not to worry, she had just been talking too much. She would be able to talk again in a week if she stayed in bed and was quiet.

The people in the kingdom heard that Queen Big was sick. They felt sorry for her, and they wanted to visit her to make her happy. They brought flowers for her. Then they told her stories. The Queen couldn't talk so she had to listen. She liked hearing the stories. Each day she got better at listening.

After one week the Queen was well. She got out of bed and dressed in her favorite dress, which was red and sparkled. Then she went outside to talk to the people of the kingdom. But now instead of just talking, she listened, too. After that she was never lonely again because everyone wanted to be her friend.

Now ask your students to open their eyes. Ask them if they saw pictures of the story in their minds while you read it. Tell them that you are going to ask them some questions about the story. Ask the following questions one by one, allowing time for your students to reach the correct answer each time.

What was the Queen's name?

What color was the Queen's castle?

What color was the Queen's Dog?

Where did the Queen's dog sleep?

What color were the houses in the kingdom?

What was the people's favorite food?

Where did the people hide when they saw the Queen?

What was the doctor's name?

What did the people bring the Queen when she was sick?

What color was the Queen's favorite dress?

Approximate Time: 15 TO 20 MINUTES

ADDITIONAL ACTIVITIES FOR UNIT 6

VISUALIZING DURING STORY READING

Read or tell stories on a regular basis. When children hear stories without seeing the pictures, they are encouraged to visualize.

STORY TAPES

Have a variety of story tapes available to play to the whole class or for children to listen to in their spare time in a listening center.

DRAWING PICTURES OF STORIES

Let children draw pictures to illustrate stories as you read them or after you read them.

VISUALIZING TO MUSIC

Play instrumental music pieces, and ask children to close their eyes and see what kind of pictures in their minds the music suggests. Classical music works well. Try pieces with various tempos and moods. Sometimes ask children to draw pictures of what they imagined.

IMAGINARY JOURNEYS

Take children on imaginary "journeys." Ask them to close their eyes, and describe in detail a "journey" somewhere, as in Activity 2. You can invoke all of the senses. You can take "jouneys" to outer space, to dinosaur times, to pioneer times, to another country, to the jungle, or anywhere you like. You can coordinate these "journeys" with your studies.

COMMERCIALLY PREPARED VISUALIZATION TAPES

Use commercially prepared tapes that offer fantasy journeys for children.

SMELLING IMAGINARY SMELLS

Ask students to close their eyes and imagine they are smelling a variety of smells. Suggest the following smells one at a time, and allow about half a minute for students to imagine each smell: cinnamon, mustard, flowers, hot chocolate, pizza, and cookies baking.

UNIT **7**

Main Idea

Introduction

Adults assume that students can comprehend the meaning of situations from a young age. Students watch situations in their daily lives or on television and make sense of them. The organization they give to a situation is one way that they comprehend those situations. One of the central skills needed to organize and understand a situation is the ability to identify and group the main ideas of that situation.

This unit includes activities that will help students identify the main idea of a situation. The main idea is the most important thing about the event or story. It can usually be summed up in one statement.

This unit begins by asking students to make choices about the most important idea in several pictures. Then it gradually works toward students drawing their own stories with a main idea in mind and asking their classmates to guess it. Finally the unit asks students to identify the main ideas from a written story.

Approximate Time for Unit 7: 85 TO 125 MINUTES

You will want to teach this unit and all of the units in more than one session, with periods of no more than 30 to 35 minutes.

There are many possible ways to schedule this unit. You might teach it in daily periods during one week. You could teach Activities #1, #2, and #3 on one day; #4 and #5 on the next; #6 and #7 on the following day; and #8 on the next. On the fifth day you might choose from ADDITIONAL ACTIVITIES at the end of the unit. You may want to include ADDITIONAL ACTIVITIES at other times during the day or use them to extend the unit into the following week.

If you choose to teach this unit in shorter periods, you could teach fewer activities each day and extend the time spent on this unit to two weeks.

UNIT 7

Main Idea

Introduction

What is this picture about?

What is the point?

The **main idea** is the most important thing or thought about a picture or a story.

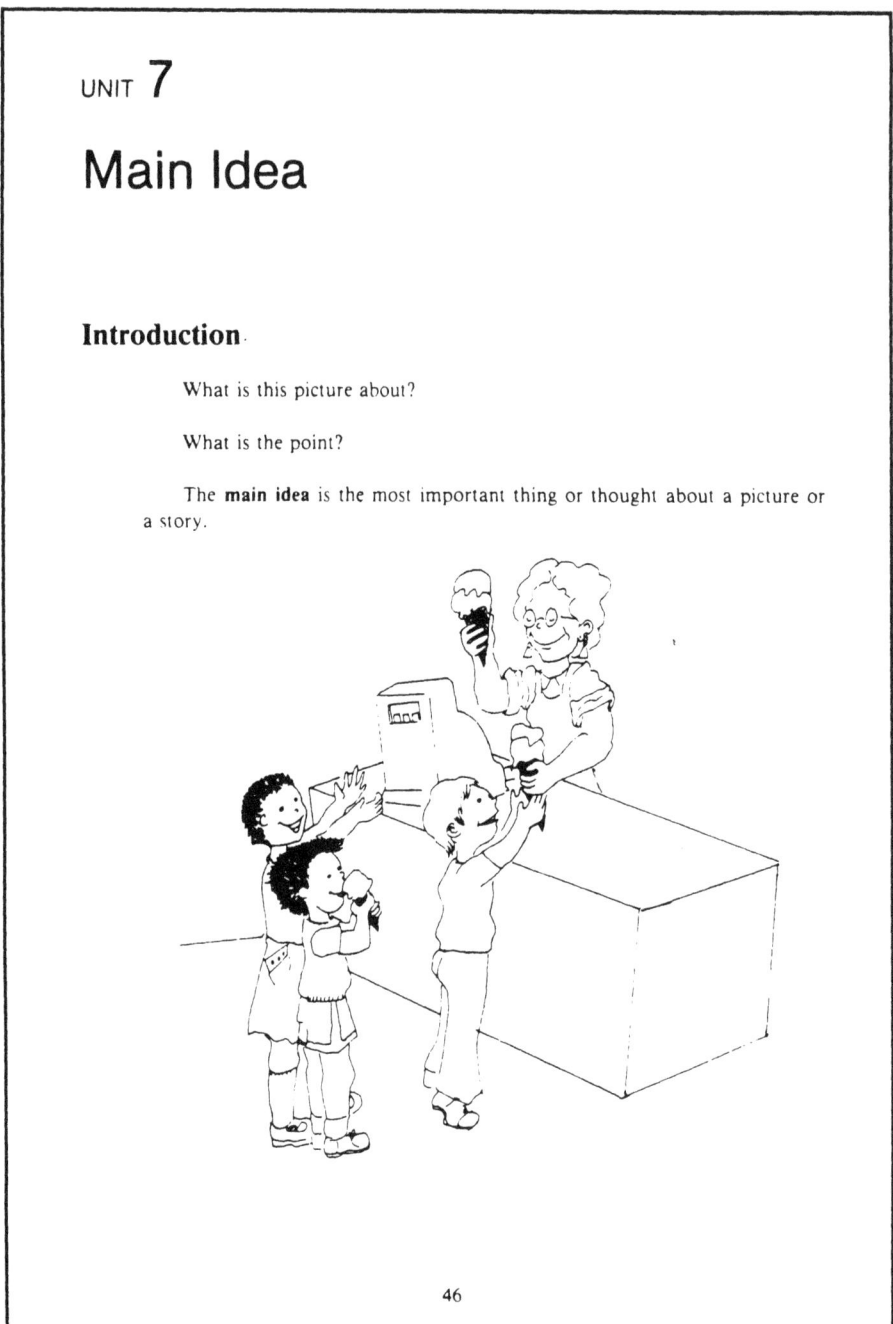

SUGGESTED ACTIVITIES FOR UNIT 7
ACTIVITY ONE: Main Point

Ask your students to turn to page 46 in their **Study Skills Programs.** Read the *Introduction* aloud. Have students identify the main idea in the picture.

Then have students recall times when they did not understand the main point of a conversation, TV show, or a story.

Approximate Time: 5 TO 10 MINUTES

ACTIVITY TWO: What's Happening?

Ask your students to turn to page 47. Ask them to look carefully at Scene #1. Ask them to think about the main idea of the scene. Give students approximately ten seconds to think about it, and then call on a volunteer to tell what the main idea is.

Do the same for Scenes #2, #3, and #4.

Approximate Time: 5 TO 10 MINUTES

ACTIVITY THREE: Choose One

Tell your students that you are going to read them a short story. Tell them that when you have finished reading, you are going to ask them to identify the main idea from three choices. Remind them that they must listen carefully so they can hear the most important thing about the story.

Read aloud story #1 slowly.

1. **Gus and his dog are friends. They help each other. Gus and his dog play together everyday. When Gus drops his pencil, his dog picks it up for him. When his dog is afraid of thunder, Gus lets him sleep on his bed.**

Then read the following aloud:

   The main idea of this story is:

   a. **The dog is afraid of storms.**
   b. **Gus is clumsy.**
   c. **Gus and his dog help each other.**

Ask a volunteer which choice identifies the main idea. Ask the students to raise their hands if they agree with this choice. Discuss why the other choices are not as appropriate.

Follow the same procedure for stories #2 - #4.

2. **Mable was tired. She lay in the grass and closed her eyes. She fell asleep. She could see other children dancing in the pictures in her mind. They had flowers in their hands and threw them in the air. When she awoke, she felt rested.**

   The main idea of this story is:

   a. **Flowers were blowing in the breeze.**
   b. **Mable went to sleep and had a dream.**
   c. **Children were dancing.**

3. The caterpillar was crawling slowly to the tree. Suddenly she heard a loud noise. A lawn mower cutting the grass came close to her head. She crept along. She heard laughter and saw a child's foot close to her head. She stopped and waited for the child to run away. Then she crawled to the tree and moved up to a branch where she began spinning her cocoon.

   The main idea of this story is:

   a. Lawnmowers are loud.

   b. The caterpillar must be careful when crawling in the grass.

   c. Caterpillars spin cocoons in branches.

4. The bluebird swooped down from the sky and grabbed a stick from the ground. He carried it to a branch and wove it with the others he had collected. Looking around he saw some straw that had fallen from the farmer's straw hat. He grabbed the piece in his beak and added it to the others.

   The main idea of this story is:

   a. The bluebird is building a nest.

   b. Farmers wear straw hats.

   c. Bluebirds can fly.

Approximate Time: 10 TO 15 MINUTES

ACTIVITY FOUR: What Is It About?

Ask your students to turn to page 48. Tell them that there is a title written above each box. Tell them that the title helps to give an idea of what the story is about. Read the title above box #1. Ask your students to draw a picture of the action described in the title. Advise students to have a clear sense of the main idea before they begin their pictures.

Follow the same procedure for boxes #2 - #4.

When students have completed the exercise, invite them to share their drawings and ideas with the class.

Approximate Time: 15 TO 20 MINUTES

3. The Terrible Day

4. We Get To The Top

49

ACTIVITY FIVE: What Is the Title?

Read story #1.

1. **George and Maria were best friends. Maria helped George learn to play wiffle ball. George shared his picture books with Maria. They shared many secrets with each other.**

Ask a volunteer to give this story a title. Ask other students for their titles. Follow the same procedure for stories #2 and #3.

2. **The day was very cold. Ephram and Zola went outside to play. First they made a snowball and rolled it in the snow to make the bottom of a snowman. Then they rolled another snowball to be the size of a head. They put it on the first snowball. They put two pieces of coal on the head for the eyes and a carrot for the nose. Then they asked their friends to come and see what they had made.**

3. **Jose and Krista were very excited. They were going on an adventure. They were going with their grandmother to the circus. They saw elephants and horses with little dogs riding on their backs. They saw ladies walking on the trapeze and lions jumping through flaming hoops. They liked the funny clowns the best of all. When they arrived home, they were very tired but excited to tell their parents about their adventure.**

Approximate Time: 10 TO 15 MINUTES

ACTIVITY SIX: Get with the Action

Organize your students into pairs. Tell them that you are going to give them a situation and they are going to act it out. Tell them that the class will guess the main idea of the action. Give each pair a situation. Some suggestions are the following:

Two friends meet on the street.

You are walking along and trip.

You hit a home run.

You pick a bouquet of flowers.

You build a tree house with your friends.

You fall down the stairs, and your mother comes to help.

You catch a fish.

Allow students several minutes to practice their action. Ask two volunteers to begin. Then have the other pairs enact their actions. After each action, ask the class to identify the main idea.

Approximate Time: 15 TO 20 MINUTES

ACTIVITY SEVEN: Create the Action

Ask your students to turn to page 50. Tell them that you want them to think of a story and then draw it in the space provided. Remind them to think about the main idea and the action before they begin. Hand out crayons to your students. Then ask them to begin. Offer help to anyone who needs assistance.

When the students have finished, ask them to title their stories. Allow students to write the title themselves, or provide assistance as necessary.

When they have completed the exercise, have your students share their drawings and ideas with the others.

Approximate Time: 10 TO 15 MINUTES

ACTIVITY EIGHT: What Is the Point?

Tell your students that you are going to read them a story. Tell them that when you finish the story, they will identify the main idea of the story. Tell them that this story has no title, so they will also need to title it. Remind them to listen carefully to the most important idea in the story.

Read the story slowly.

In a small village, there once lived a small girl named Toshi. She was not rich, but she was kind. She never harmed any living thing. She could not pick the flowers in the fields because they lived with the other flowers. She could not catch fish from the sea because she liked to watch them swim away.

One day a stranger appeared in her village. He was carrying a snake in a bag. He needed seeds to grow food to feed his family, but he had no money. All he had was the snake that he carried in the bag. Not one person in the village would trade some grain for the snake. Toshi could not bear to see the snake in the bag. She gathered her few coins and gave them to the stranger in exchange for the snake. The stranger could then buy grain. He thanked Toshi and gave her the bag.

Toshi bowed and carried the snake to the ocean's edge. She looked closely at the beautiful snake. She felt sorry for the animal. "I cannot keep you," she said. So she let the snake go.

A few weeks later, Toshi was visiting the castle with her class. They saw beautiful paintings and gardens. They saw jewels so bright that it hurt their eyes to look at them. But they also saw guards with stern faces and very sharp swords. Toshi approached one of the guards and asked, "Why do you stand so big and tall?" "I am guarding the Princess," he replied and shoved her off her feet and onto the floor. At that moment the Princess appeared to inquire about all the noise while she was trying to work. The guard informed her that this little girl was trying to break into the sacred room. The Princess asked Toshi her name and, upon hearing it, smiled, bent down, and softly helped her to her feet. The Princess left without saying a word.

Toshi started to walk slowly from the palace to join her class. She glanced down at her hand which the Princess had held and stopped short. There on her hand was a picture of the snake.

Toshi could not understand what had happened. She returned to her village and walked to the sea. She looked at the ground as she walked and found that she could see right into the earth. There were bugs burrowing their way through the ground and little rabbits asleep in their holes. When she got to the water's edge, she could see oysters asleep in their shells. She looked closely and saw one shell with a sparkling piece. She could see a very large pearl in the shell. She waded into the sea and dug the shell from the sand.

The pearl was worth many riches. Toshi was able to provide seeds to use for growing food for everyone in her village.

One night, Toshi heard a noise at the door. When she looked up, she saw the princess standing there. The princess said, "I know that you are now happy, and I need to give the gift I gave you to another. You no longer need it." The princess took hold of Toshi's hand. She patted it twice and walked out the door.

Toshi looked down at her hand, and the picture of the snake was gone. She rushed outside to see the princess. But the only thing she could see was a beautiful snake by the ocean's edge. The snake slithered softly into the darkness, never to be seen again.

Ask volunteers to identify the main idea of the story. Students may be able to give several different main ideas depending on their level of thinking. Some students may say that the main idea is that oysters have pearls. At a more abstract level, students may say that the main idea is that kindness will be rewarded. Encourage students to talk about their ideas.

Ask students to suggest a title for the story.

Approximate Time: 15 TO 20 MINUTES

ADDITIONAL ACTIVITIES FOR UNIT 7

READING ALOUD

Develop your students' understanding of main ideas by reading them passages, poems, and other selections aloud. Have them articulate the main idea of the passage they have heard.

FILL IN THE BLANKS

Have students fill in words in a cartoon strip or a picture that has action. Let them tell you what is happening.

PICTURE FILE

Have on hand a file of pictures that you can refer to. Ask students to identify what is happening and how they know.

COMMERCIALLY PREPARED MATERIAL

Weekly Readers or other newspapers provide an excellent format for discussing main ideas. Alternate between having students read the titles with you and tell what the article is about, and having them read the article with you and tell what the title might be.

FAMOUS PAINTINGS

Show students prints of famous paintings. Ask them to give each painting a title.

WORDLESS BOOKS

Show the students pictures in a wordless book. Have students give the book a title. They can also dictate a script or text for each page to go with the title.

UNIT 8
Creative Problem Solving

Introduction

The ability to find new solutions to problems is an essential one for students growing up during a period of ongoing change. Students need to learn how to look at problems from different perspectives and bring fresh and creative responses to them. Your students will use their ability to develop new and varied solutions to problems not only in their classroom work but in all areas of their lives.

This unit presents a number of different approaches to problem solving to your students. These approaches promote creativity, flexibility, and enhanced decision-making skills. In each of the approaches, students are encouraged to think of many possible solutions to problems rather than one "right" one. In some of the exercises, students are also asked to evaluate their solutions to decide on the most effective ones.

Approximate Time for Unit 8: 135 TO 190 MINUTES

You'll want to teach this unit and all of the units in more than one session, with periods of no more than 30 to 35 minutes. You could teach activities #1 and #2 on the first day; #3 and #4 on the next day; #5 and #6 on the third day; #7 and #8 on the fourth day; #9 and #10 on the fifth day; and #11 on the sixth day. Alternatively, you could teach fewer activities on each day and extend the unit over two weeks. You may want to include ADDITIONAL ACTIVITIES at other times during the week or extend the unit into the following weeks.

UNIT **8**

Creative Problem Solving

Introduction

You **solve problems** every day, both in and out of school.

This means that you find answers to questions or think of different ways to do things.

Creative problem solving means being able to find many new answers to questions or many new and different ways to do things. The activities in this unit will help you do this.

SOLVING A PROBLEM

What do you see in the picture?

Can you help Louis and Maria solve their problem?

51

SUGGESTED ACTIVITIES FOR UNIT 8

ACTIVITY ONE: Solving Problems

Ask your students to turn to page 51. Read aloud the *Introduction*. Then read aloud the first question in *Solving a Problem*. Invite responses. When your students have described the situation in the picture, read aloud the second question. Explain that no one is allowed to criticize anyone else's ideas. Ask for suggestions.

Allow students to offer as many ideas as they can think of, one at a time. Write them on the blackboard or on a large sheet of paper. If only a few ideas are suggested, you can suggest others to stimulate your students' thinking. When students have finished, praise them for all the different solutions to the problem that they generated.

Approximate Time: 5 TO 10 MINUTES

BRAINSTORMING

What do you see in this picture?

This woman has a "storm in her brain." She is **brainstorming**.

This is a funny way of saying that she is thinking of many good ideas to solve a problem.

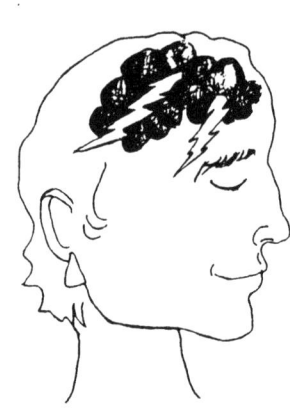

What is this? **Brainstorm** all the things you could do with it.

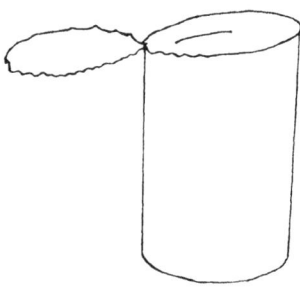

ACTIVITY TWO: Brainstorming

Ask your students to turn to page 52. Look at the pictures, and read aloud the sentence at the top of the page. Tell students that "brainstorming" is a way of finding as many new ideas as possible. Tell them they have already "brainstormed" in the first activity, when they thought of all of the ways that Louis and Maria could get apples from the tree. Tell students that the rules of brainstorming are the following:

1) Let your mind be free to think of whatever ideas it wants to think of. Don't worry if these ideas seem funny or strange. Sometimes the best ideas seem funny and strange at first because we're not used to them. Of course, the ideas don't have to seem strange. They can be any ideas at all.

2) Don't criticize your ideas or anybody else's ideas. When you are brainstorming, you are trying to think of as many ideas as possible. You are not trying to decide which ideas are right or best.

(You might want to write a short version of these brainstorming rules on the blackboard or on a poster before class.)

Now ask students to look at the picture on the bottom of page 52. Read aloud the words above the picture. Ask students to name the object in the picture. When they have identified it as a can, tell them that the can is empty. Explain to your students that they are now going to brainstorm as many things as possible that people can make or do with an empty can.

Allow student to brainstorm ideas. Write their ideas on the blackboard or on a large sheet of paper. Encourage students to think of as many ideas as possible. You may make suggestions to help stimulate new avenues of thinking. When students have thought of as many ideas as possible, praise them.

Approximate Time: 10 TO 15 MINUTES

ACTIVITY THREE: Brainstorming about Random Things

Collect ten random objects, such as a button, a spool, a box, a book, a piece of paper, a shoe, an apple, a ring, a hook, a clothespin, and a paper clip. Hold up one at a time, and ask students to brainstorm different uses for each object, as they did with the can in the last activity. Do not record responses. Encourage students to respond quickly. Focus on each object for about one minute. You may want to encourage students to suggest other objects in the classroom.

Approximate Time: 10 TO 15 MINUTES

ACTIVITY FOUR: The Magic Squares

Ask students to turn to page 53. Ask them to identify what they see on the page. When someone has said "squares" or "four squares," acknowledge that as correct. Then hand out crayons or magic markers.

Say to students: **"I want you to pretend that you each have magic powers. You can use your crayons/markers to change the squares into anything you can think of. First brainstorm in your own mind as many things as possible that you could turn your squares into. Let's have a few suggestions."**

Allow several students to offer suggestions. Illustrate one of them on the blackboard.

Then say: "**Now think of other things quietly to yourself. Use your crayons to change the squares into whatever you want. Remember that there are no right or wrong answers. If you can't think of things to change all of them into, or you don't have time to finish, it doesn't matter. There are no right or wrong answers. Take as long as you like on each square, and work until I tell you to stop.**"

Allow students to work on this for five to ten minutes. When a student seems to be done, go to her/him and talk about her/his changes. If a student seems to be having a hard time thinking of ideas, work with her/him to generate some.

Then have each student share with the whole class one of the things into which he/she "magically" changed a square.

Approximate Time: 15 TO 20 MINUTES

ACTIVITY FIVE: Silly Questions

Tell your students that you are going to ask them to answer some questions that might seem silly. Explain that these are questions that will help their minds to think in new ways. Tell students that there are no right or wrong answers.

Then select from the following questions, and ask them one at a time, eliciting as many responses to each as possible. Choose as many questions as you like, but select at least four or five to give students practice with a variety of questions. You may write answers on the blackboard if you wish.

1. How would the world be different if everyone were one foot tall?

2. How would the world be different if everyone had an extra set of eyes on the back of their heads?

3. How would the world be different if everyone stayed up all night and slept all day?

4. How would the world be different if people could breathe under water and lived under water?

5. What would it be like if you could hear people's thoughts?

6. Which is happier, a cow or a tree? Why?

7. Which is stronger, love or hate? Why?

8. Which color is faster, red or blue? Why?

Approximate Time: 15 TO 20 MINUTES

ACTIVITY SIX: What Could Be Happening in This Picture?

Ask your students to turn to page 54. Read aloud the words on the top of the page. Ask students to look at the picture at the top of the page. Explain that you want students to take turns telling what might be happening in the picture. Note that different students may think different things are happening, that there are no right or wrong answers. Invite students to respond, and write their responses on the blackboard or on a large sheet of paper.

Then ask students to turn to page 55. Repeat the procedure as above.

Approximate Time: 10 TO 15 MINUTES

WHAT COULD BE HAPPENING IN THIS PICTURE?

Think of different things that could be happening in this picture.

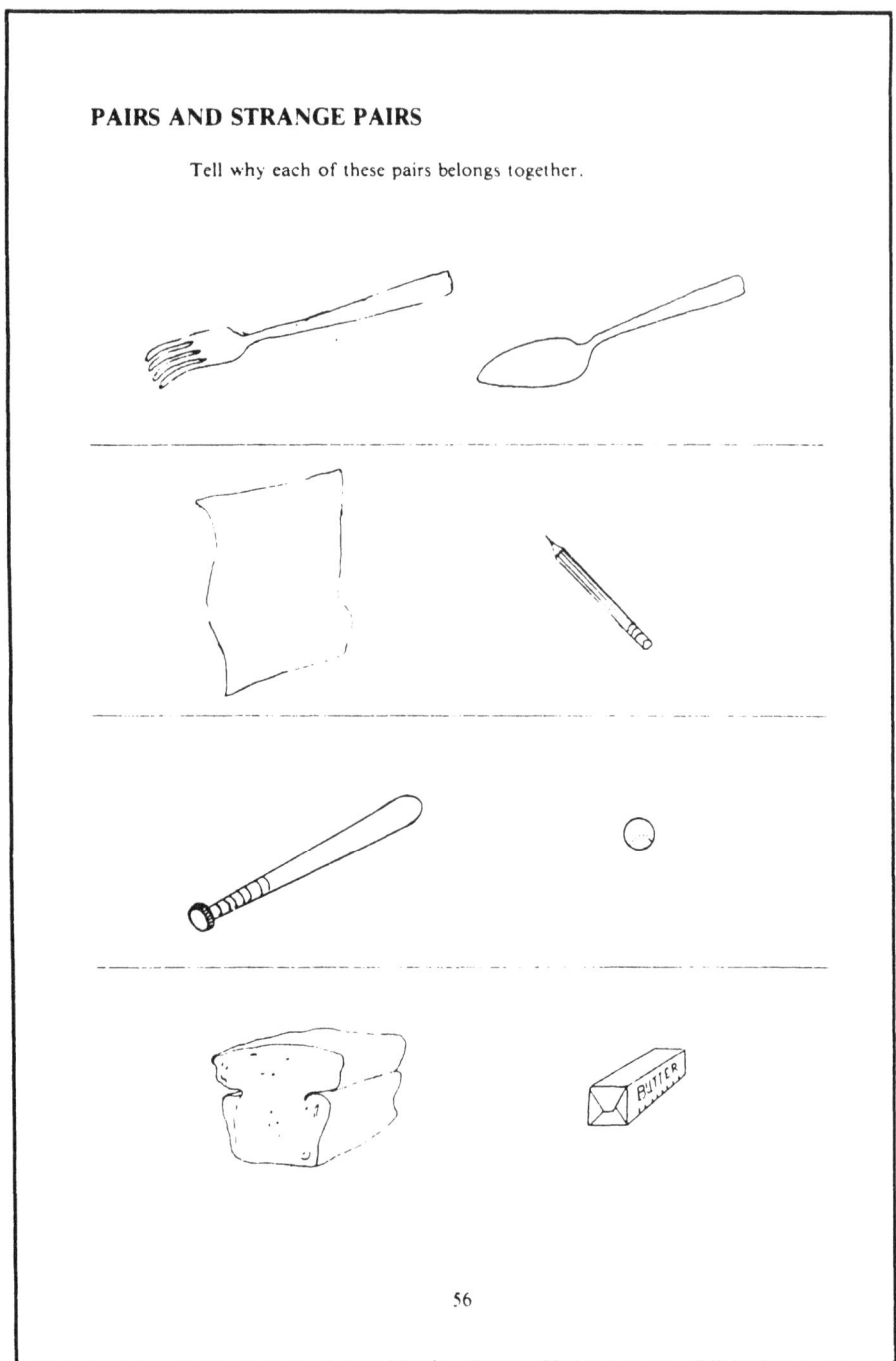

ACTIVITY SEVEN: Pairs and Strange Pairs

Ask your students to turn to page 56. Read aloud the title. Ask your students to explain what a "pair" is. Then read aloud the directions at the top of the page. Ask your students to look at the pairs of pictures and tell why the items in each pair belong together.

Now ask your students to turn to page 57. Tell your students that these are pictures of strange pairs. Then read aloud the directions at the top of the page. Ask your students to brainstorm reasons why the two pictures in the pair might be alike or how they could fit together. Tell your students that the reasons may seem funny or silly. Say that each person might think of a different reason why the pictures might fit together.

Use the first pair of pictures as an example. Ask students to identify the lemon and the ball. Then ask for reasons why they might be alike or fit together. If students cannot think of any, offer suggestions, such as "You could fit them both in your pocket," or "You could play catch with both of them," or "Both of them could be yellow," or "A dog could chew on both of them," or "You could roll them both on the ground." Wait until students have offered as many suggestions as possible. You can write the responses on the board if you wish.

Go on to the next pair. Repeat directions with each pair.

Approximate Time: 5 TO 10 MINUTES

PAIRS AND STRANGE PAIRS

Think of reasons why each of these pairs could belong together.

ACTIVITY EIGHT: Magic Wand

Give your students the following directions: **"We are going to play a game. I will pretend that I have a magic wand. When I wave the magic wand over you, you will change into other things. After you change into something else, you will first pretend to be that thing and then tell me about how that thing sees the world.**

"Now we will try the game. Watch me wave my wand. I have just turned you all into apples. Pretend to be an apple. You can curl up round in your chair, like an apple, but you must be quiet and hold very still. Think about what the world would be like for an apple. Hold still for a moment until I wave my wand again." (Pause for about thirty seconds.) **"Now I'll wave my wand and turn you back into yourselves."** (Wave imaginary wand.) **"Turn back into yourself. Now I'd like you to tell me what it's like to be an apple."** Allow children to share the point of view of an apple. Accept whatever they say.

Now give the following instructions: **"This time when I wave my magic wand, you will each turn into a rabbit. You are a rabbit locked in a small cage, just the size of your chair, and you can't get out of your chair. You can wiggle your nose and smell like a rabbit, and you can pretend to wiggle your ears and hear what a rabbit would hear. Remember that rabbits are very quiet, so don't make any noise. Think about how a rabbit would see this room. Now I'll wave my wand."** (Wave imaginary wand, and pause for about thirty seconds.) **"Now I'll wave my wand and turn you back into yourselves."** (Wave imaginary wand.) **"Turn back into yourself. Now tell me what it's like to be a rabbit locked in a small cage."** Allow children to share the point of view of a rabbit. Accept whatever they say.

Approximate Time: 10 TO 15 MINUTES

INVENTING MACHINES

This is a strange machine.

What do you think this machine could do?

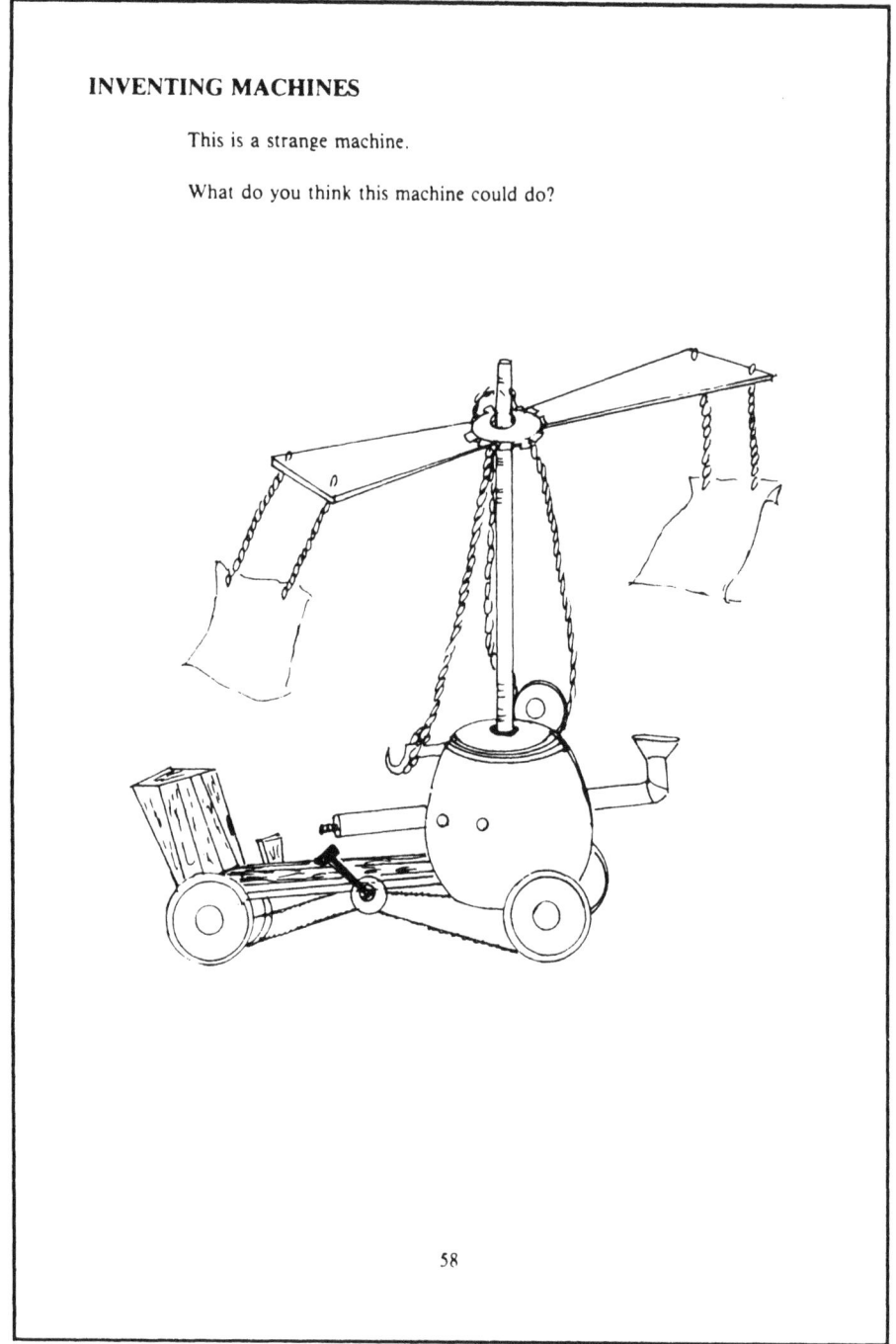

58

ACTIVITY NINE: Inventing Machines

Ask your students to turn to page 58. Read aloud the sentences on the page. Ask students to think of ways that the machine might be used and to tell why. You might give an example such as the following: "I think it's a machine to squash cans flat because it could roll over them." Give each student who desires an opportunity to contribute one idea.

Now ask students to turn to page 59. Read the words at the top of the page aloud, and ask students to describe the picture. Explain that Alice's parents have told her she must finish her work before she can go outside and play. She must hang up her clothes, make her bed, and pick up her toys. Ask students if they can invent a machine that will be able to do Alice's work for her so that she can go outside and play. Be sure that your students understand what "invent" means. Tell your students that the machine can be any kind of machine.

Give students a pencil and a supply of crayons. Read aloud the directions on the bottom of the page. Allow about five minutes for students to draw their machines.

When students have finished, ask them to find one or two partners with whom to share their machines. Praise the students for the many kinds of machines invented.

Approximate Time: 15 TO 20 MINUTES

INVENTING MACHINES

What do you see in this picture?

Draw a machine to do Alice's work.

ACTIVITY TEN: Brainstorming about Real Problems

Ask students if they remember what "brainstorming" means. Review the two rules: that any idea can be suggested, and that no student is allowed to criticize any other student's ideas.

Tell your students that you will be brainstorming about problems that might come up for them at school or at home.

Read aloud the following: **"The first problem happens outside on the playground. There is only one swing left that has nobody using it. Two students get to it at the same time. They both grab it and start arguing about who should be the one to use it. I want you to brainstorm some ways that they might solve this problem."**

Allow students to brainstorm as many solutions as possible. Write them on the blackboard or on a large sheet of paper.

Then say: **"All of these ideas are good ideas. Now we will look at why they might or might not work well to solve the problem if it happened on the playground today."** Go over the ideas one at a time. Have your students explain why an idea might or might not work well. Do not let students make fun of any of the ideas.

Read aloud the following problem: **"A group of students is playing softball near one of their houses. One of them accidently hits the ball on the roof the house. It stays on the roof. They want to get it down so they can play. Let's brainstorm some ways to solve this problem."** Follow the same procedure for brainstorming and evaluating as in the previous example.

Now either think of a problem that is occurring or has occurred recently in your classroom or school that students could brainstorm solutions about, or choose one that seems relevant from the suggestions below. Repeat the procedure.

Students want to learn about a certain subject, such as circuses, pioneers, or space travel. Brainstorm activities that could help them learn about it.

Brainstorm ideas about how to cut down on lost articles of clothing in the classroom.

Brainstorm ideas about how to arrange for classroom pet or plant care over vacations.

Brainstorm ideas about fair ways to take turns with classroom jobs.

Approximate Time: 15 TO 20 MINUTES

ACTIVITY ELEVEN: Creative Dramatics with Problem Situations

Tell students that they are going to work together in small groups to dramatize and solve problems. Explain that they will share their problems and solutions with the rest of the class.

Assign students to small groups with four or five members. Give each group one of the "problem" situations below, or think of others. Ask each group to brainstorm solutions and then to decide on the best solution. Help them to dramatize both the problem and the solution. Work for a few minutes with each group to help the group members plan how they will dramatize the situation.

Allow each group a short time to enact its drama for the rest of the class. You or a student in the group should explain what the problem and the solution are before they are dramatized.

SITUATIONS:

A family comes home from the movies and discovers that they have lost their keys and are locked out of their house. What can they do?

Some children want to play together, but each one wants to play a different game. One wants to play ball, one wants to play tag, and one wants to climb trees. They begin to argue. How will they decide what to play?

A family owns a dog. When the family goes away to work and school, they leave the dog in the back yard, which has a fence around it. One day while the family is gone, the dog digs a big hole under the fence and runs away. The family comes home and discovers that the dog is missing. They call him, but he doesn't come. What can they do?

Astronauts on the moon discover that their space ship is broken. How will they get back to earth?

Explorers in a strange country come to a high wall that does not seem to have a beginning or an ending. How will they get over wall?

Hikers are lost on the mountain, and it is getting dark. What will they do?

Approximate Time: 20 TO 25 MINUTES

ADDITIONAL ACTIVITIES FOR UNIT 8

AMBIGUOUS PICTURES

Find pictures from newspapers or magazines that could have different interpretations of what is happening. Mount them in the classroom with the question: What different things could be happening here?

Or find pictures where one thing is clearly happening, and cover up part of the picture. Mount them in classroom with the question: What could be happening here?

WHY GAME

Begin by asking children a "why" question. In response to each answer, ask another "why" question. Keep going until the process naturally stops or until you run out of time. Example: "Why do children go to school?" "Because their parents make them." "Why do their parents make them go to school?" "Because they want them to learn." "Why do they want them to learn?"

Other questions: Why do we usually build square or rectangle houses instead of round houses? Why do people have two ears? Why do horses sleep in barns?

COLLECTING WALK

Take a walk to look for all kinds of objects to collect. When you get back, look at objects one at a time, and brainstorm about their possible uses.

MAKING UP ENDINGS TO STORIES

Find or write a very short story. Read it to the class, leaving out the ending. Ask students to make up different kinds of endings to the story. This is an activity that can be done and enjoyed regularly.

INVENTING WITH ART OBJECTS: GENERAL

Keep a supply of "beautiful junk" art construction materials in your classroom. These can include the following: toilet paper and paper towel tubes, pieces of paper and cardboard in different shapes and sizes, boxes of all shapes and sizes, buttons, cloth cut in various shapes and sizes, paper bags, ribbons, disposable food packaging materials such as aluminum pie tins, egg cartons, and anything else you can think of. Ask parents to help supply you with these items. Also keep a variety of construction materials available, such as paper clips, glue, rubber bands, scotch tape, and masking tape. Allow students to make their own creations with these materials.

INVENTING WITH ART OBJECTS: SPECIFIC

On some days, give each child certain art materials, such as the following: one toilet paper tube, one paper bag, one bow, two buttons, and three different kinds of paper. You can give different sets of objects to each student. Also allow access to glue, tape, scissors, and so on. Announce a theme for the day, such as robots, monsters, funny cars, or machines. Ask each student to make one of these objects from the materials you have given her/him.

PAPER BAG DRAMATICS

Divide the class into groups of four or five children. Give each group a paper bag containing four or five miscellaneous objects, which they will use as props in a skit that they make up and present to the class.

NOTES

NOTES

NOTES

NOTES

NOTES

NOTES